A MAKEOVER FOR LIFE

MARION CREEDON HEGARTY

CONTENTS

This Book is Dedicated to the Two Men in my Life:

To Cormac, my darling husband, my soulmate and my best friend. Thank you for being in my life and always being there for me. To Tom, my darling son, my boy, my world. You were my 'why', my reason to live!

ACKNOWLEDGMENTS

I wish to express heartfelt gratitude to Dr Tony Humphreys for his wisdom and insightfulness. Tony, you have shared some incredible life secrets, inspired my spiritual growth and helped me to find kindness and compassion for myself and others.

To Mary Groeger and Jane Jolly, my soul sisters whom I have known since my first day in Miss O'Sullivan's Secondary School. We've been through good, bad and indifferent times together, and we've always been there for one another. Thank you for your unconditional love.

Mary, thank you as always for your ever-supportive presence, and for your reflective feedback and words of encouragement during the writing of this book.

To my 'shovel buddy' Helen Casey. It's great to know if I ever have to kill someone, you'll bury him with me and tell no one. And you know I'm ready to return the favour! We've been on such a similar journey, and somehow, we survived it through laughter and tears. I think I've talked with you every day of the last thirty years or more. Thank you for being a great friend.

To my wonderful friend and former neighbour in Grange Erin,

Helen Hogan. We've both had our struggles, and we've always had each other's back. Thank you, Helen, for being an important part of my life.

I want to send grateful thanks to my wonderfully supportive West Cork buddies, Mary O'Brien, Kathleen Leonard and Eileen Connolly and the Cork city friends I've known and loved forever, Joan Horgan, Eleanor Goggin, Mary Hayes, Maura O'Brien and Patricia Lynch.

A note of thanks too to Mary McMahon, my friend from Ennis in Clare and to the wonderful Creagh family, Richard and Shirley and Billy, Daisy and Calum. I love you all. A special note of appreciation to my much-adored nephews Alan, Kevin and Paul Goggin and to my friend, Alan Leonard, an inspirational young man whom I greatly admire. I owe many thanks too to my great friend and solicitor, Patrick Goold in Macroom.

Cormac and I have so many other good friends, family and incredible neighbours in our lives including Mary, Bernard, Sean and Aishling Kelly, Jack and Eileen Leonard, Pat and Ann Leonard and Michael Joe, Brian, Stephen and Julie Ann Leonard.

Much love and appreciation too to Marcella Creedon, Marie and Noel O'Brien and John and Deirdre Cashell and to all my awesome friends and colleagues from U.C.C.

There are so many other beautiful people, too many to mention, who I've been privileged to meet on my life's journey.

Wishing all of you love, peace and joy.

Marion Creedon Hegarty

INTRODUCTION

My name is Marion, and as a young woman, I was devastated by so much grief and tragedy, that I didn't think I would survive it.

Struggling to find a new direction in life, I discovered a career in style and image consulting. It was through this work that I discovered a deep love for helping my clients unwrap the beauty that lies within all of us. I can honestly say that inspiring others to look and feel their absolute best saved my life!

My training and experience in the fields of beauty therapy, cosmetics, colour analysis, image and styling are extensive. But equally important are my studies in self-growth and personal development, which helped me to heal my grief and become a happier and better person.

Thanks to university qualifications in interpersonal communications and relationship mentoring, I acquired the life skills to develop a 'mind' makeover plan that expanded my beauty and image training.

Assisting positive change in others' lives has been much more than a job to me. It has been a life-long and enduring passion. It lights me up from the inside to be able to enhance, empower and enrich other people's lives!

A makeover can reach far beyond the clothes and make-up that we wear. It is not just about colour, fashion, make-up and grooming or about body image coaching and style analysis.

A makeover is something broader and more inclusive. It's about acquiring a greater understanding and appreciation of our divine selves. It involves a life makeover that is both physical and psychological and helps us feel better and more confident about ourselves.

My makeovers also include self-growth and social skills such as interpersonal communication, table manners and etiquette. They include practical life tools and techniques acquired from thirty-five years of experience and learning.

I love to help everyone shine with confidence in every situation and become our most capable and charismatic selves from the inside out.

I also like to encourage everyone to move beyond our perceived limitations and help us to achieve our true potential.

For more than three decades, I have been guiding others to become their very best selves, and I believe I have developed a Makeover for Life programme that is both holistic and powerful.

Now after a lifetime in makeovers, I have decided to write this book to share my journey, experiences and knowledge. This is a book that is part-autobiographical and partly, what I hope will be a transformative self-help guide.

My journey has been painful and tragic in parts, but it has also filled with love, kindness and blessings. It has taken hard work inside and out to get to the peaceful, happy place I am in now and to realise that my most important relationship is the one with myself.

I hope that by sharing my story of loss and survival, it can help guide others who experience tragedy and suffering in their lives.

And I hope that by sharing what I've learnt over decades working in image, style and personal development, that I can impart valuable life knowledge and insider trade secrets to help many others.

Making a positive difference in others' lives makes my heart sing. So, in the following pages, I impart the most valuable insights I have learnt down the years; a kind of compendium of all the wisdom I wish I had known when I was starting out in life.

At the same time, this book is not prescriptive. Every person on this planet is uniquely wonderful as they are. And I would never presume to know more about anyone else's life and their lifestyle than they do. This is merely a book of suggestions and guidelines which I have found personally transformative and which have helped me and many of my clients experience life with greater ease, happiness and fulfilment.

My hope is that A Makeover for Life will inspire you, the reader, in your life. My book - like my journey and my lifetime's work - is about facilitating positive change and making each day easier and simpler for all of us. And I believe I am living proof that the increased confidence and joy this can bring about is truly life-changing!

PART I
MY LIFE MAKEOVER

Me in Corfu after our engagement.

THE ACCIDENT

The night before the accident, Friday 13 May 1983, I had no idea that the wonderful life I shared with my husband was about to end.

I think of us sitting there in our kitchen, talking late into the night, oblivious to the fact that time was running out for us.

In Corfu after our engagement, 1979.

I felt depressed and despairing, suffering from the effects of a late miscarriage two weeks earlier. It was a lack of information. If I had known that the turmoil of emotions I was experiencing was normal, I could have coped better. I didn't understand why I couldn't just 'get on with it' like everyone else apparently did.

'Why am I not feeling better, Tom?' I asked him. 'Why do I still feel this way?'

My husband was reassuring and gentle as always.

'Marion, I hate to see you go through this, but you'll feel better soon. We'll put this behind us, you'll see. Focus on what we have - a wonderful boy and a lovely life together.'

I can still see him that night, tall, athletically built with a shock of soft-brown hair and warm blue eyes. To everyone else, he was Tom Creedon, the outstanding inter-county Cork footballer. To me, he was my loving husband of two-and-a-half years and a doting daddy to his son.

The miscarriages were the only clouds in our happy life together. I had the first less than a year after baby Tom arrived. It was an early one, but it was upsetting. We were elated when I fell pregnant again and looked forward to a brother or sister for our boy. I was four months into the pregnancy, driving home from the post office after collecting the children's allowance when I had a near miss on the road. There was no collision, and I got more of a shock than anything. My concerns at the time were about our twenty-month old son, Tom, who was in the car with me. But by the time I got home, I had started bleeding.

I lay in bed in the General Hospital in Ennis for a week, as they tried to save the pregnancy. For a whole week, I stared up at that peeling grey paint on the ceiling, hoping against hope that I wouldn't lose our baby. I remember Tom was playing in a football championship for Macroom while I was in the hospital. He was the captain, so I urged him to go to the match.

'I'm going to be fine, Tom,' I said. 'You have a job to do, so just go do it.'

The phone rang beside my bed that afternoon, and it was Tom to tell me they won the game. He was delighted, and it was a massive coup for him as captain, so I was happy for him.

'I'm on my way back to the hospital now,' he said.

'No, stay where you are,' I said. 'I'm grand here. You're the captain. You are needed in Macroom, so stay and be part of the celebrations.'

I remember poor Tom arrived at the hospital the next morning with bloodshot eyes and his face red from drink. He had a copy of the Cork Examiner under his arm.

'Look, it's all over the paper about our win!' he said.

He was trying to distract me and hoping to cheer me up. But I remember thinking, *Will you f*** off with your newspaper? I don't give a damn about your match.* I didn't say it out loud, but I never felt like that before. I was in such a black place then.

I was losing the baby, and I was gutted, really depressed. It was the first time I felt this darkness, this terrible gloom. No one talked about postnatal depression in those days, and I was probably feeling the impact of the earlier miscarriage on top of this second one. Women were expected to move on and forget about miscarriages in those days. They were non-events, and no one mentioned them. But I was grieving, and I remember feeling so low during those days. And I hadn't emerged from that darkness when I lost Tom.

The night before the accident, we continued talking. Tom was due for football practice in Cork the next day, and afterwards, we were to attend a corporate dinner for his work.

Tom's passion was football, but his day-job was working as a civil engineer building the ESB's new Moneypoint coal-fired power plant in Ennis, County Clare. We were living in Ennis to be close to Tom's job, but most weekends we travelled back to Cork for Tom's GAA fixtures.

Tom, always a kind soul, wanted to make me feel better.

'Why don't I bring the baby with me to Cork tomorrow?' he suggested. 'I can leave him with your mum while I go to the game, and you can have some time to yourself for a change. You could get your hair done for the dinner tomorrow if you wanted.'

He said he planned to borrow a van from one of the guys on the Moneypoint site to collect a new suite of furniture delivered to my parent's garage in Cork. With Tom Junior already walking, our lovely cream suite was no longer practical, and we had ordered a darker, more hardwearing suite.

The next morning, I waved Tom off with his gleeful child, who loved any excursion with his dad. Then fifteen minutes later, as I sat down with a cup of tea, Tom reappeared at the door again, flustered.

'You won't believe this,' he said. 'I forgot my gear bag!'

I burst out laughing because he was more liable to forget me than his precious bag of football gear. He enjoyed seeing me laugh, and as he was rushing out the door again, he paused to say, 'Hon, I love you. I'll see you this evening.' It was like he was sent back to say a final farewell. They were his last words to me.

I went into Ennis to have my hair done, and then I met my friend, Una, for coffee. A couple of hours had passed.

'Why don't you come back to the house for an hour or so?' she said. 'Tom won't be back for ages yet.'

So, I got into my car and followed her to her house. When we got there, we saw a Cork registered car abandoned in the middle of the road. I started laughing. 'You have visitors from Cork and look at how they've parked the car! You know, that could be my mother - she got a new car this week!'

I was joking, but Una's front door swung open as we reached it, and my father was standing there. Una's husband, Ciaran, was hovering behind him, and I wasn't sure, but it looked like he had been crying.

'What's up?' I asked, stunned to see Dad there.

'There's been an accident. The van rolled backwards,' he said. They are the words I heard. The world stopped for an instant, and my heart began banging with fear.

'Is the baby, okay? Is my baby, okay?' I asked, my eyes darting from my dad to Ciaran. Dad was instantly calming. 'Your baby's fine,' he said. 'But Thomas is in hospital, and he's looking for you. I came up to Una's to see if you were here. We'll drive down to Cork together.'

He was vague; he didn't seem to know what exactly had happened except the baby was fine, and Tom had to be brought to the hospital because 'the van rolled'. I saw my brother-in-law Billy then, and I thought it was odd because he was ashen-looking, and he wasn't saying much either.

'I brought Billy so he could drive your car to Cork with us,' said Dad. He had thought of everything.

Una lived in a bungalow, and I remember going into a bedroom inside the front door and sitting down on the edge of the bed. I sensed there was something more, something they weren't telling me.

'Is Tom going to die or something?' I said to Dad.

He didn't appear panicked at all and just rolled his eyes.

'For God's sakes, we're all going to die. Can we get going?'

He seemed calm, and his demeanour reassured me.

'Okay, but I have to go back to the house and collect all the fruit we bought yesterday. I don't want it to go to waste in case we have to stay in Cork for a few days.'

I know it sounds crazy that I was concerned about fruit, but I was thinking, *Okay, the van rolled backwards and hit a wall, but if the baby is okay, my big, strong, healthy husband is surely okay.*

The drive back to our house in Ennis took ten minutes, and I went into the kitchen and started packing the fruit.

'Billy and myself will do that,' said Dad taking over. 'You just pack a few things.'

'Do you think we'll need much? Will he really be in the hospital for more than a day?' I asked. 'How much should I bring with me?'

'Ara, bring what you need now,' Dad said, 'and sure we can come up during the week if we need more.' He was such a rock. The only indication that I got that maybe things weren't great was when Dad started talking almost to himself during the two-hour journey to Cork.

'It's so sad because that man is just a gentleman. And he loves his boy, his wife, his job and his game of football. And you know, he never did anybody any harm.'

'Dad, why are you talking like that? It's just an old van,' I said. 'It just rolled back and hit the wall, right?'

'Well, you know,' he said. 'I'm not even sure myself what happened.'

He was trying to save me for as long as he could.

When we reached Cork city, Dad asked, 'What do you want to do, love? Will we head straight for the hospital?'

I said, 'No, I want to see the baby, and then we'll go in.'

I knew there was something they weren't telling me. I wanted to reassure myself that Tom Junior was okay. When we arrived at my parent's house, I found all my sisters, my brother and their partners in the house. A neighbour was carrying Tom in her arms.

I could see immediately that our child was fine, but I wondered about my family. They were a noisy bunch, and there wasn't a word. I went into the kitchen to make myself a cup of tea, and my sister Celine came in and said, 'Ah Marion, don't bother with the tea. I think you should go to the hospital now.'

'Really?' I said. I still didn't think that Tom could be in any danger. How bad an accident could it be if our baby was fine after it?

My family didn't want to tell me; they were all so protective. They may have been hoping for a miracle before I got to see him. So, I hadn't a clue what I was facing as I walked in the door of the Cork Regional Hospital. I only got inside the hospital when I recognised a face, somebody from the GAA. I can't remember who he was now, but I remember saying to him, 'Did you hear that Tom had an accident?'

I saw the shadow that passed over his face, and he said, 'I know Marion, I'm really sorry.' It was that man's expression and the tone of his voice that alerted me. For the first time, I thought, *Oh, Jesus!*, and I ran through the hospital then. Someone, I don't know who, led me to intensive care. *Intensive care? What is going on? How could Tom be in intensive care?* My mind was a jumble of confusion and terror.

The moment I saw him was like a full punch to the gut. He was lost amid wires and blinking machines, attached to life support and beeping monitors and surrounded by the sound of tubes pumping and whooshing. His body was hugely swollen, and his head was almost wrapped entirely in a massive bandage. I barely recognised him.

'Tom!' I shrieked in horror. His eyes flew open for just a second, bloodshot and unfocussed, and then they closed. I ran to him, tried to talk to him, but there was no response. I went out and told everyone that his eyes opened, but they shook their heads and said I imagined it. His eyes opening is something I will never forget.

I remember almost pleading with the doctor, 'Is he going to be all right? Will Tom be all right?' I didn't have a clue of the extent of his injuries. 'Twenty-four hours will tell a lot, and forty-eight hours will tell more,' is all the doctor would say.

I didn't know at that stage that Tom had already been resuscitated three times and was fighting for his life.

It seemed impossible that the lifeless and devastated body, which lay in that hospital bed was the same vital man who had told me he loved me just hours previously, and the same man who had been the heart of my life for the previous five years.

From the very first time I laid eyes on Tom, there is no other way for me to describe it except *love at first sight.*

The day I met him started like any other. It was spring 1979, and I headed for the Grafton Health Studio on Lower Oliver Plunkett in Cork, where I had been working as a beauty therapist for several months. The studio was a state-of-the-art health complex, the only one of its kind in Cork back then.

Beauty, fashion and style were my obsessions from the time I was a child. My parents paid for me to follow my dream and attend the renowned Jill Fisher's Beauty College in Dublin after leaving school.

Jill was a very elegant London-trained beauty specialist. She worked in the salon of the exclusive Claridge's Hotel, a second home for Hollywood and British royalty before she set up in Dublin. After training with her in Dublin, I also modelled part-time with Carmel O'Gorman, who ran an agency and deportment school in Cork.

So, when a vacancy arose for a sales representative and consultant for Mary Quant, it was the perfect job for me. I was nineteen years old, and I flung myself into the work. I loved my job. As part of the work, you would see me promoting in the window in Switzers of Dublin or Cash's of Cork in my Mary Quant crinoline dresses with their huge ballgown-style skirts. I did make-up shows, demonstrations and consultations all over the country.

After a couple of years on the road living out of a suitcase, I was burnt out. The gloss of the job was fading for me. When a friend said she was going to America for the summer, I decided to go too. I learnt even more about the make-up business while working on the cosmetics counters of the big department stores in America.

When I came back to Ireland at the end of 1978, I moved back into Cork's quiet and leafy suburbia with my mum and dad, Denis and Sheila Goggin. I felt a bit aimless, not knowing what I wanted to do. I knew I wanted to stay in Cork.

That was when my great friend, Jane Jolly, the manager of Grafton Health Studios, offered me a job. A notice was placed in the Examiner in November 1978 reading: *Grafton Health Studios are pleased to announce that Marion Goggin has now joined our staff as a beauty therapist and Kwik-slim consultant.*

Everyone in the studios was young and enthusiastic, and we took turns to work on reception. I was behind that reception desk one day, when the man I was going to marry arrived into my life. All I can say is that all the oxygen seemed to leave the air when I first laid eyes on him. His skin was tanned to a shade of mahogany, and his hair was tousled and sun-bleached blonde. He was so handsome, but had a quiet and shy demeanour. It was a very attractive combination, and my heart beat faster as I took his details for membership.

I learnt that his name was Tom Creedon, he was twenty-four years old and a recent graduate in civil engineering from University College Cork. He worked for the big civil engineering group, Ascon and had just returned after several months in Africa working under a broiling sun on his first construction project, which explained his deep tan and flaxen hair.

He may have said something about football or being in the GAA that night, but I knew nothing about sports or football. We were never a sporting family. My dad was an avid fisherman, and he always had a little boat for fishing, but football and GAA was a foreign land to me. I didn't know at that stage that Tom Creedon was a high-profile figure in the GAA world.

I waited until he had left before turning to my friend Jane with a gasp.

'Oh my God. Did you ever see anyone so handsome, and he's single?'

It was a couple of weeks before I saw him again. Tom gave me a nod and a shy smile and disappeared into the squash courts with his playing partner. *He's too shy,* I thought. I could either wait forever for him to ask me out or take matters into my own hands and ask *him* out. I chose to do the latter. I don't remember the details, but I'm sure it involved red faces and awkwardness. I know we arranged to meet in the pub, Dwyer's, on Dawn Square in Cork, for a first date.

Meeting him that night, I was full of nervous anticipation. But once our eyes locked, it was like we were the only two people in the world. We were totally absorbed in one another. Mary Morgan, a woman I knew for years, happened to be in the pub that night with her husband, Billy Morgan. Billy captained Cork to win the All Ireland football finals in 1973 after a lapse of twenty-eight years. Inevitably, Billy and Tom spotted each other and started talking, and that's when Mary came over to me and hissed, 'What in the name of God are you doing with the likes of Tom?' Her reaction to my date shocked me. *I knew he had to be too good to be true. What's the matter with him?* I panicked.

It turned out that Mary meant she would have never matched me with a GAA player. It was true. I'd never been on the sidelines of a match in my life. I knew nothing about his world. And yet, we both fell in love that night, and that was it. We really did.

At first, he was so quiet that it was hard to gauge his innermost thoughts. I wondered if he felt as strongly about me as I did about him. Then on our second or third date, he said: 'You're so beautiful. Why aren't you in the movies?' He said it in all earnestness, and that was when my heart soared. It was then that I knew for sure that he liked me as much as I liked him!

I soon learnt that Tom was an exceptional GAA footballer. He first came to prominence as a member of the Cork minor team that won the All-Ireland final in 1972. He also wore the green jersey of Macroom where he revitalised the fortunes of his beloved club. Soon after, he donned the blue jersey for Munster and the red colours of the Cork senior team.

Tom played in every Munster final from 1975 and was much-loved and admired by all who knew him. Of course, I became an ardent Cork supporter and watching him on the field, I couldn't have been prouder of him. He was a superb athlete, and he played with heart and passion.

As a couple, we were different in many ways. While he was quiet and reserved, I was more outgoing and social. He was from Macroom, born in the middle of a large family with four sisters and two brothers. My family were very much city people. I was the eldest of four sisters and one brother who lived in a comfortable semi-detached house on Murmont Lawn in Montenotte.

In some ways, however, we were very similar. We shared the same values and morals and respected marriage, family and religious devotion. We valued trust, commitment, communication, hard work and ambition. Very quickly, we also realised that we shared a vision for the future, one where we'd both be together, forever. The truth is that we were smitten from the very beginning. He adored me, and I adored him.

He was sharing a flat over the other side of Cork city when I met him, but he quickly moved to a flat closer to my parent's house so we could spend more time together. I remember how my heart lifted every time I laid eyes on him. It was the seventies, so no one had much money, but we still had a great social life, most of it connected to the GAA.

Tom proposed about six months after we met. It was at the wedding of fellow Cork footballer, Seamus O'Sullivan to our friend, Mary, in the Church of the Immaculate Conception in Clonakilty in November 1979.

I didn't hang around for Tom to change his mind. We went down to Reilly's Jewellers' on Oliver Plunkett Street in Cork where our budget was limited to a small amount in savings. Normally, I loved dramatic clothes and statement jewellery, but for our engagement, I knew I wanted a simple ring, something classic and timeless.

'I want a ring with one stone to represent the two of us becoming one,' I said emphatically.

So, we picked out a diamond solitaire together. It was only a chip of a diamond, but to me, it was worth more than Elizabeth Taylor's sixty-eight-carat rock from Richard Burton. I was so proud to wear his ring.

We needed to save for a house, and I knew I could earn far more as a sales representative on the road than as a beauty therapist. So, I left the Grafton Health Studios and began to work for Irish Pharmaceuticals. I was on the road most weekday nights, but Tom would always come and

Tom and me on our wedding day September 24, 1980.

meet me wherever I was on a Wednesday night. We started viewing houses and planning a wedding for the following year.

For me, the priority was my wedding dress. I found the perfect wedding dress in the Pronuptia bridal collection, but I couldn't afford it. Instead, I found a fabulous dressmaker and asked her to copy the perfect dress. The white gown was long and flowing with gorgeous Swiss lace that my mum and I bought in Arnotts department store in Dublin. It was off-the-shoulder for the evening but had a white cape for the church.

We got married on Wednesday, 24 September 1980, within eighteen months of meeting. My dress was gorgeous, everything I dreamt of, but my hair, usually my pride and joy, was a disaster. We did my hair at home. The thought of going to the hairdressers on the morning of the wedding didn't even enter my head. My mother tied my hair in rags overnight to curl it. I woke up the next morning and shook out the rags to reveal a headful of tight ringlets and spiral curls. 'It's like a cross between a Shirley Temple wig and a bad perm!' I wailed, but there was nothing that could be done at that stage. I wore a wreath of silk flowers on my head, which my mother bought in a bridal store in London. I also had a trailing white veil, but my hair tortured me that day.

I remember when I reached the altar of Saint Joseph's Church on Old Youghal Road, Tom reassured me, as he always did.

'You look gorgeous, just gorgeous,' he said, his eyes soft and adoring, even though my friends' eyes popped when they saw the state of those spiral ringlets. My hair only began to soften that evening. By about seven or eight o'clock that night, I felt relieved. My hair was back down to my waist in lovely soft waves again. Ours was a big wedding with close to two hundred people attending the reception in the Blarney Hotel on the outskirts of Cork city. We both had big families, lots of friends and then there was the GAA factor. We had a lot of people to invite.

Kerry had been the thorn in Cork's side in the Munster finals for years. Tom played in nine Munster finals, including two replays, losing each time to Kerry. It was the seventies and eighties, the era of the Kerry greats.

Me and Mum on my wedding day to Tom

Kerry won four straight All Irelands finals between 1978 and 1981.

Despite the great rivalry, Tom's favourite song was the Rose of Tralee, and it became our song. I remember Tom going up on stage the night of our wedding to serenade me. It took courage to perform in front of everyone because he was a quiet man, but it was important to him to sing it. I joined him on stage as he sang the final chorus: *She was lovely and fair as the rose of the summer. Yet, it was not her beauty alone that won me. Oh no! It was the truth in her eye ever beaming, that made me love Mary, the Rose of Tralee.* My heart swelled with love for him.

I was the happiest bride that day, and Tom's eyes shone with love for me. We had found our other halves. I didn't think I could have loved him more that day, yet my love for him deepened again after we married. We were so happy then. We were in

Me and dad, Denis on my wedding day

our twenties, healthy and in love and had our whole lives ahead of us. The world seemed like such a golden place. Everything was so perfect, and when you are young, optimistic and blissfully happy, you never think anything can take that away. I was so naive. I had no idea that all those dreams we held for the future would be so easily shattered.

My dad, Denis Goggin, Tom's mother Majella, his father
Tom Creedon and my mother, Sheila at our wedding
September 24, 1980.

SIXTEEN WEEKS

*a*t Cork Regional Hospital, I gradually began to piece together what had happened and how my husband was on life support in intensive care.

It was around lunchtime that Tom went to collect the suite of furniture which had been delivered to my parents' house in Cork.

My parents' house was on an incline, and Tom parked on the road outside. He always taught me to put the car in neutral when I stopped the car, so I imagine that's what he did that day. Our baby was in the front passenger seat, and Tom started to pile the furniture into the back of the van. The weight of the furniture must have triggered the van to move, and it began rolling backwards down the hill.

I believe pure instinct kicked in when the van carrying Tom's defenceless child began to roll down the hill. I know Tom would have happily given his life to protect his boy. He ran after the van, got behind it, and tried to stop it, but he must have slipped. Whatever happened, he was run over and trapped underneath, and the heavy van dragged him one hundred and thirty feet until it struck a wall.

He was resuscitated at the scene by a passing ambulance man after they managed to lift the van off him. A Southern Health Board ambulance rushed him to the North Infirmary Hospital where they resuscitated him twice again. Then they transferred him under garda escort to the Regional Hospital in Cork. Tom suffered multiple injuries all over his body, and the skin was shorn from his back. But it was the head injuries that were the problem. They told me he had a brain stem injury, but I didn't have a clue what that meant at the time.

On the following Monday, forty-eight hours after the accident, I finally met with Tom's neurosurgeon, Mr Michael Feeley. He shook his head sympathetically. 'I'm sorry Marion, but Tom is not going to survive this.' I gazed at the man in complete shock, before I broke down in tears, devastated. I was a frightened, terrified young wife and mother, whose world had been turned upside down in a matter of hours. But I truly, honestly believed that Tom wouldn't die. I argued, pleaded and tried to make him say the words that I wanted to hear – that Tom would recover in time. But the consultant offered no hope.

'Marion,' he insisted finally. 'He's going to die. You know that, don't you?'

I didn't believe for one minute that Tom would die. I felt he loved his son and me too much for him to leave us. I thought that love could cure everything.

'No, he won't, doctor. I'm telling you; he's going to come out of this, and he'll be fine," I said. I said it with complete conviction.

Within days, they took Tom off life support. He seemed to wake after a few days, but he only made simple reflex movements. They said he was in a vegetative state and hearing the word 'vegetative' applied to someone I loved was very difficult but the term is still used today.

All I know is that his eyes opened at times, and that was enough to give me hope. They moved him into the GA Neurosurgery ward. He was in a ward with six beds where all the patients suffered severe brain injuries from traffic accidents, aneurysms and brain haemorrhages. The only sounds in the room came from the medical staff and the visitors - the patients were nearly always still and silent.

Our son was the light of Tom's life and as soon as my husband was stable, I brought the baby to him. I knew that if anything could bring Tom out of that vegetative state, it would be the sound of his baby boy calling him.

We discovered I was expecting within three months of our wedding, and neither of us could have been happier. We both wanted a baby more than anything, and once the doctor confirmed the results of my home testing kit, we were thrilled. I felt I had everything I had ever dreamt about – a husband I adored and a baby on the way. All my dreams had come true.

We even had our dream house, a new modern house near Douglas in Cork. My parents gave us the deposit for our first home. We didn't have any money to furnish or decorate the place, but we felt privileged to be able to start married life in our own home. Tom designed and built the stone fireplace himself, and we put down carpets. We moved in with whatever small bits we owned. My mother had given us a dining suite as a wedding present, and we had a couch and one or two lamps and a bed. That was pretty much all we had.

Married life was even better than I could have hoped for, and I had the highest of expectations. Tom gave me so much love. The only way I can describe it is that he just adored me. I just felt so loved and protected. We both worked hard, but we were happy.

Around the same time that I discovered I was pregnant, my company, Irish Pharmaceuticals, went into liquidation and Tom's employers promoted him and transferred him to Ennis in County Clare. They wanted him to work on building the ESB's new Money-point coal-fired power plant outside Ennis town.

It seemed like all the stars were aligned for us. My job was gone anyway, and I was expecting our first baby and moving to Ennis meant that we could continue married life on our own, away from everyone. It was just the two of us starting up a new life again. We were embarking on a new adventure, and we loved it.

We rented out our first house in Grange Erin in Douglas to an English couple, and Tom's company gave us a generous allowance and expenses to move to Ennis, where we rented another house and set up our new life together. Tom enjoyed his new job, and we were both eagerly awaiting the arrival of our baby.

Our baby's due date came and went six months later, so the doctors decided that I was to be induced. We went to the Bon Secours Maternity Hospital in Cork together first thing on Tuesday morning, 29 September 1981, almost a year to the date after our wedding. I loved being pregnant, every minute of it, but I was scared out of my wits about the birth. I was so apprehensive that I brought a Black Madonna statuette, said to protect pregnant women, into the hospital ward with me.

Tom settled down by my bed prepared for a long wait. He must have bought every newspaper you could buy in the country, and he started leafing through the sports section of all of them.

Me, Tom and baby Tom.

That evening, I was still in labour, the baby hadn't budged, and Tom and I were wild-eyed and scared. Everything started to happen quickly as soon as the medical staff realised our baby was in distress. I found myself being whisked off to surgery for a caesarean section.

Tom was the first to hold and cradle our baby. He was already madly in love with our son before I ever laid eyes on him. I was drifting in and out of consciousness after the procedure, but I recall Tom holding that baby possessively. I remember he kept telling me: 'He's so handsome. He's the image of me!' Even in my dazed condition, I was astonished. Tom was the humblest of men, so unassuming, and here he was rhapsodising about how beautiful his baby was and how this beautiful baby was the spit of him. I can still hear Tom saying, 'Look, Marion, isn't he beautiful? Isn't he the image of me?'

Tom with two of his favourite things - his baby and his
football, Lahinch Clare.

Tom Junior was a huge baby, just shy of ten pounds - nine pounds
and ten ounces to be exact. He's six-foot, four inches tall today, so
you can imagine. He was a thumper of a new-born, fine and healthy
and strong. Tom Junior was also the first Creedon grandson. He
was the new generation of Tom Creedon, the third or the fourth in
a line of Tom Creedons.

I remember trying to come to terms with the fact that this baby's
head was completely bald. He didn't have a rib of hair. And I
remember how besotted Tom was with his son. He couldn't be
persuaded to put that child down, telling me over and over how
gorgeous he was. It began the instant he held his son in his arms. He
was mesmerised by him; he worshipped that little boy; loved him,
absolutely loved him.

In those days, women were kept in the hospital quite a long time after a caesarean, but Tom was determined to stay with us. He slept on the chair beside my bed and refused to go home. I remember the gynaecologist, Robin O'Donoghue, arriving in on the second day and saying, 'Tom, would you at least go home and change your clothes?'

'I don't want to leave her on her own,' said Tom.

'Please, go home. She'll be fine. We'll look at her,' said the doctor.

Tom the father with Tom the son.

'I'm asleep most of the time anyway!' I said. 'Go home and get some rest!'

Tom, Santy, Baby and Me.

So, he went home, and I reckon he called into my parent's place for half an hour because when I woke up, he was back beside me again.

I think it was about the fourth day after the birth that he had to go back to work. He worked every day in Ennis in County Clare, but he drove two hours back down to Cork and two hours back every night so that he could see us after work.

I didn't think it was possible, but after the baby arrived, we were even happier. Tom rushed back from his job every evening to be with us. His life revolved around the baby, me and football. He was such a rounded, solid and grounded man whose family was everything to him. He was fantastic with our son. He couldn't get enough of the child and revelled in his every tiny milestone and achievement. He wanted to be home with us all the time.

Every photograph of Tom Junior as a boy has him brandishing a football. The child was drop kicking a ball at fifteen months. When the accident happened, and everything fell apart, football disappeared out of his life for a very long time.

The day that I brought our baby to the hospital for the first time after Tom's accident, I was filled with a sense of nervous excitement. That child was so important to Tom that I was convinced once he heard his boy calling to him that he would come around. I really did.

I can never forget Tom's ward. It was modern, but all drab beige with flimsy curtains separating each bed. The only natural light came in a window down the far end of the room which I think overlooked the Wilton Shopping Centre. Tom's bed was immediately inside the door on the left, so I rarely looked out that window. I carried our baby into that dull ward brimming with hope and optimism.

'Look Tom, look! It's Daddy! Look at Daddy!' I said. Tom Junior responded like I knew he would and started clapping and calling out for his daddy. I had been so sure that when the baby called out to him, Tom would respond. I was absolutely convinced there would be some sign of recognition. But my heart began sinking because there was nothing, no reaction at all. Tom lay inert and unresponsive, lost somewhere even beyond his precious child's reach.

I spent most waking minutes with Tom in the early weeks. But as time went on, I began spending the mornings with Tom, afternoons with the baby in my parents' house, and then I'd come back to the hospital again in the evening until around ten o'clock.

Sometimes, it was as if Tom seemed to recognise my voice because his head turned and followed me as I talked. That was the only response to stimuli that I could discern in him all those months. I never knew if he recognised my voice or if he was responding to the most familiar voice around him. I waited, hoped and watched for any other sign of conscious awareness. I kept hoping and believing he would break out of the dreamlike state he appeared trapped in.

His bedside became my family living room for the next sixteen weeks. They were sixteen weeks when we could have had many quiet hours together, but instead, I remember a constant stream of visitors, many of them strangers. It was an open ward and people, some just random GAA fans, kept coming.

I just wanted to be alone with my husband. Instead, I had to make conversation with people I didn't know, and who didn't know me. The constant swarms of visitors were stressful and exhausting, and some people were overbearing. But I was young and didn't know how to set boundaries. I should have only admitted those close to us and asked other people to leave us in peace and to pray for him instead. If anyone is ever in a similar position with an ill family member, I would suggest that they establish a boundary from the start. Appoint someone close as a gatekeeper or ask the hospital reception to restrict visitors. I wish I had the knowledge then, that I have now because I just wanted to spend time alone with my husband.

There were some visitors and friends who, of course, were always welcome. Tom's friend, Seamus O'Sullivan, travelled down from

Limerick at least once a week to see him. He was such a loyal friend, a wonderful man, one of several mutual friends who I loved to see arrive. It was great to remember all the good times and the experiences we had together, and I hoped that these conversations could reach Tom and somehow stimulate him and help in his recovery.

Tom and I had enjoyed a great social life over the previous years. We had the best of both worlds moving between Cork and Ennis every week. We spent five or six nights a week in Ennis. On Friday or Saturday nights, we came to Cork for Tom's football match at the weekends. We would stay with my mum and dad, and they would get to dote on their grandson for at least one night a week.

I always looked forward to meeting the other girlfriends and the wives after each match. Mary O'Sullivan, Eileen Kehilly, Mary Morgan and Frances Allen were among a supportive group of women I met with all the time. We were all the same age, and many of us had new babies, so we had a lot in common.

Tom was an extraordinarily quiet and reserved man, and I loved that about him. I loved his gentleness. He was a strong man also, but very quiet, very softly spoken. Yet, we'd have a few drinks and go dancing and have great fun together. I loved that I was able to make him smile, and we laughed a lot together. I remember one of Tom's friends marvelling at the changes in him after we met. 'All I can say is you brought him to life!' she laughed.

I thought about what she said, and I still believed that I could do it again. I thought that his son and I could bring him to life again. I just would not accept that Tom was gone from us. On rare occasions when I was alone with my husband, I'd hold his hand, talk to him and play him his favourite music. I played those beautiful John Denver hits to him, songs like Take Me Home Country Roads and Rocky Mountain High. I would also read the sports pages to him every day.

But still he didn't respond to what was happening around him, and I wasn't sure if there were ever signs of conscious awareness. I kept telling myself to be patient, and I expected him to come around and open his eyes and speak to me at any moment.

'He just needs time and rest, and he'll recover. I know him. Tom will fight his way back, just watch,' I said. God, help me, I was young and naive. Instead, I watched my poor husband deteriorate in front of me. I saw him die slowly, bit by bit of him fading away until there was just a shell of the man in that hospital bed.

Anyone in that traumatic situation requires love and compassion and kindness. It's so important to have people who will hold you and listen. I was very blessed to have that love and compassion from my family and friends. Their soothing care eased the terrible emotional trauma of those days.

My mother and father were amazing, looking after my baby when I was in the hospital and looking after me when I came home. Many friends came to sit with me in the long hours, and they offered a respite from streams of people I barely knew coming to Tom's bedside.

Marian Toner, who has since died, was a wonderful support. She would make me laugh during times so dark that I felt I'd never laugh again. She was gorgeous, a fantastic friend and a beacon of light during the blackest of times.

The nursing staff couldn't have been kinder or more compassionate too. They were devoted in their care for Tom and became like a second family to me, especially the night nurses because they weren't as busy as the women on the day shift. I remember one night having a cup of tea with one of the nurses. I had arranged a collection of family photos on Tom's locker, including a lovely portrait of my husband.

'Marion, do you see the man in the photo and the man in that bed?' she said. 'Don't you see that the man in the picture is gone?' I was shocked and hurt by what she said. Of course, the woman was only trying to warn me that Tom was dying, but up until the end, I

28

believed he would come back to us. No one could persuade me otherwise.

It was unthinkable to me, incomprehensible that he wouldn't recover. I was in total denial, but as I understand it now, it was total fear. I couldn't face the truth; it was too hard to bear.

Tom's survival against the odds gave me hope too. He seemed to defy all the medics' predictions, and he continued to live week after week. The truth was that had been so athletic, so healthy, fit and strong to begin with, that his body refused to die.

I remember my parents begged me to take a break from the hospital and to go away for a night. 'Stay with your aunt - it will be so good for you to get away,' my mother said. 'You need to get out of the hospital.'

Even though it was just one night away, I thought I would lose my mind if I didn't get back to the hospital. I just wanted to be with him in case he woke up and was looking for me. I always applied make-up and wore my nice clothes every morning in the hope that this would be the day.

But as week sixteen approached, the nurse's words were sinking in. I began comparing the photo of Tom and the man who lay in the hospital bed, and in the end, even I couldn't fail to miss that he was fading. I began to have the first inkling that maybe I was wrong. Maybe, Tom wasn't coming back. On the Thursday before he died, he had a bad day and needed a lot of care and attention from the staff. It was a horrendous day, very stressful. I went home that night, but I felt a nagging feeling that I had to go back.

It was after eleven o'clock, and I sat beside the bed again, tears pouring down my face. I was quiet because I always avoided crying in front of Tom. I tried to sound positive around him. I hoped that he was sleeping, silently getting better, and one day he would hear us and respond again. But I was despairing now, and the hopes I'd held in my heart for his recovery were fading. While I sat there in the quiet of the ward, I realised with a shock that there were tears rolling down Tom's face too. I always hoped that he wasn't suffering, and now I couldn't be sure.

'You can go, love,' I told him. 'You can go. You've suffered enough. Your dad will look after you. Just please try and look after Tom and me where ever you're going.'

Still, Tom clung on to life.

That Sunday, 28 August 1983, saw the replay of Cork versus Dublin in the All Ireland semi-finals in Páirc Uí Chaoimh. Our friends said, 'Come on, Marion. You have to come along. You could do with the day out, and you can tell Tom all about it when you get back.'

So, I visited Tom in the morning, told him where I was going, and I went to the match in the afternoon and watched Cork being defeated again.

After the match, I was heading down the hospital corridor to Tom's ward, when one of his nurses ran to me and stopped me. I can't remember her name now, which is unfortunate, because she meant such a lot to me during all those appalling months. Her expression was grim, and she held my wrists and tried to make me understand. 'He's gone, Marion,' she said. 'I'm so sorry, but Tom's dead.'

I stared at her in absolute shock and despair. I couldn't believe that I hadn't been there with him in the end. I was blinded by tears, grief and frustration, and I remember getting so cross with her. I had to hit out at someone. 'You were supposed to look after him when I wasn't there!'

I remember his poor mother, Majella, arriving around the same time, distraught with pain and shock. God love her, she had only lost her husband a year earlier. At least Tom would have been happy to see the deep, loving bond Majella had with her grandson in the years after his death.

But that night, all I remember was feeling so lost, terrified and dazed. My heart was thumping in my chest. I was a very young widow and a petrified one. My beautiful husband had died less than a month short of our third wedding anniversary.

How could Tom have left us? How am I going to rear our boy on my own? Can this really be happening...?

SURVIVAL

 uch of those hideous months during Tom's illness and the grim months after his death are a dark blur. I have snapshots but very few really detailed memories of the time. It's not surprising. I've since learnt that memory loss is a defence mechanism which helps us to protect ourselves from the worst depths of traumatic events. It helps us to cope by allowing us to avoid some of the overwhelming emotional, psychological and physical feelings associated with tragedy.

By the time Tom died, I had wasted away to six-stone in weight. My eyes were shrunken in my skull, and I looked twenty years older than I was. I looked like an old woman at the funeral.

By divine providence, our family friend, Father Galvin, happened to be covering for the hospital chaplain the night Tom died. People were looking at me to decide funeral arrangements, and I was reeling. I felt adrift, floating around in shock. I wasn't capable of making any decisions. And suddenly appeared the familiar and comforting face of Father Galvin, a man who had spoken at our wedding.

'Do you know what I suggest you do?' said Father Galvin. 'Why don't you have the removal and funeral in the church where you were married? Then take Tom back to Macroom to be buried.'

I nodded in agreement. It was a relief to have a plan.

'I think I want to do that,' I said. Tom was devoted to his local football club, Macroom. He was passionate about the team and his teammates. So, I decided to lay him to rest in Macroom near his dad and his beloved club.

Tom's removal and funeral were huge events attended by many people; thousands of people. I remember so many nameless faces, and I wondered at the crowds. I also remember sitting in that church and staring at Tom's coffin at the altar and feeling that this was unreal, grotesque. We had been married at that altar less than three years earlier, and we had been so happy. And there was Father Corkery, the priest who officiated at our wedding, celebrating my husband's funeral mass. It felt like I was trapped in a nightmare that I couldn't wake up from.

I recall seeing the nurse who had told me that Tom died. We gazed across at one another in the church, and I felt her love and sympathy. I just have these vague recollections and brief instances from the days of Tom's removal and funeral, but I didn't really know what was going on.

A lot of what I know about those days was gleaned from the newspapers afterwards. I read how the Dublin team stayed in Cork and attended Tom's funeral along with his Cork teammates. The Lord Mayor of Cork, the GAA president and many GAA officials and members of the public paid tribute to him during those days.

I don't recall that long twenty-seven-mile journey from Saint Joseph's Church in Mayfield to Saint Colman's Cemetery in Macroom where we laid Tom to rest. However, I can never forget the awful sight of my husband's coffin being lowered into the ground. That terrible moment stands out in stark relief my mind. I swayed, my legs barely supporting me. I couldn't believe that my beautiful man, the father of our child, was gone.

I also remember yearning for my baby, feeling an overwhelming need to hug him, smell him, hold him close to me. But I had left the baby at home for Tom's funeral, because everyone said I should, and I regret that to this day. It would have been so much better to have had him there because I needed him to hold on to. He was only a year and eleven months, but I would have loved to have him with me on the day of his father's funeral.

During those days and the subsequent weeks and months, I remember the endless loneliness, the sick hollowness in my stomach and the unbearable ache in my heart.

We had bought a house in Ennis, but we didn't have mortgage protection on it because we already had a policy on our house in Cork. So, I sold the Ennis property, paid off the mortgage and moved back into our first house in Grange Erin with the baby.

I wondered if I would ever get used to going home with the baby to an empty house. Or if I'd ever get used to never seeing Tom again. I kept expecting him to walk through the door in the evening for his dinner. I had to stop myself putting on extra potatoes and food for Tom. Every time I saw an idle football around the house or garden, my heart lurched in pain. I thought about how Tom would never take his son to a match, how he would never be there for his first day at school and how we would never be together as a family again.

Tom, aged 4, presenting the Tom Creedon cup to Tim Healy,
captain of the O'Donovan Rossa team. Far left is Con Murphy
of the Cork County Board and me, standing far right.

I didn't know of anyone who went for counselling in those days. Nor did I consider taking prescribed medication because it would have been like a public admission that I couldn't cope. Grieving people were told: 'Get on with it, and get over it.' It was over a decade later before I went for counselling. But I was lost in a fog of grief, pain and distress, which was overwhelming at times. There were many times I wanted to die myself, and it was only the love of our baby that kept me going.

I found it hard very hard being around our mutual friends, the people we knew and loved in the GAA. Meeting with them without Tom brought back too many memories. I didn't understand the waves of anguish that I felt, and so I tried to avoid anything that brought me pain, including those mutual friends.

I remember I went on a holiday to Spain two months after Tom died. It was just the baby and me, and I think I hoped that when I got on that plane that I'd leave the pain behind. I arrived in our hotel room in Marbella, and the first thing I saw was a bottle of bubbly and two glasses on the table. God, it felt like another cruel blow, and I bawled and bawled. It was just another reminder that the life we had was never coming back. The loneliness I felt was bottomless; the anguish, endless.

Meanwhile, the GAA community rallied and honoured Tom by donating a cup in his name soon after he died.

The Tom Creedon Cup.

Many years later, in 2004, Tom Junior and I were also proud to be present for the opening of Tom Creedon Park in Gurteenroe in Macroom.

It was also a great source of pride when the Cork poet and the Oxford University-based academic, Bernard O'Donoghue, penned the most beautiful poem, Munster Final, in Tom's honour.

Munster Final

The jarveys to the west side of the town
Are robbers to a man, and if you tried
To drive through The Gap, they'd nearly strike you
With their whips. So we parked facing for home
And joined the long troop down the meadowsweet
And woodbine-scented road into the town.
By blue Killarney's lakes and glens to see
The white posts on the green! To be deafened
By the muzzy megaphone of Jimmy Shand
And the testy bray to keep the gangways clear.
As for Tom Creedon, I can see him still
His back arching casually to field and clear.
'Glory Macroom! Good Boy, Tom Creedon!'

We'd be back next year to try our luck in Cork.
We will be back next year, roaring ourselves
Hoarse, praying for better luck. After first Mass
We'll get there early; that's our only hope.
Keep clear of the carparks so we're not hemmed in,
And we'll be home, God willing, for the cows.

For a long time after my husband's death, I was lost and aimless. I had my baby, and he was my priority and my only reason for getting up in the morning.

I had a deep faith, but after Tom's death, I drifted away from it for a while. I was angry. I thought, *why did this happen to us? What did we ever do to deserve that? Why did God let a good person like Tom die?* I was confused, disillusioned and sad and wondered, *what is the point of all this?*

Socially, I became fearful and lonely. I had supportive family and friends, but my heart was broken. I had been living a dream, and now it was all gone. My confidence in life, my optimism and my hope were shattered. I was back out in this strange world of being single again, and my grief felt endless. I never drank at home, but every weekend, alcohol became my release. I was in horrendous pain, and drink became something to ease the pain and give me a feeling of confidence again. I dropped the baby to Mum and Dad on a Friday or Saturday night, and I would go out with friends. Every Sunday, I went home and back home to normal life, but I looked forward to those weekend nights when I could drink and obliterate all the darkness and pain in my life.

That first Christmas after Tom died was like being trapped in a nightmare. I felt like I was going to lose my mind as I was surrounded by carols, jolly snowmen songs and festive cheer. It seemed as if I was struggling to stay alive, yet a massive party surrounded me. Each of these events and milestones came at me like one blow after another. Birthdays were about celebration, Valentine's Day was about romance, anniversaries were about sharing, and I felt like I faced all of these on my own. Tom's loss felt like my limbs had been brutally torn from me. I really believed that I would be like this forever; that I would never feel real joy and happiness again. My life was drained of all colour and vibrancy, apart from the light that was my boy.

I remember talking to a good friend's husband, a child psychiatrist, who assured me the darkness would lift.

'Marion, you only see blackness now but believe me, there will be a time soon when you'll see glimpses of greys. It may go back to black again, but you will start seeing more and more grey. And then in the middle of all this grey and black, you'll see a streak of white or light. That will grow too, and then you will have a drop of black, a bit of grey and a lot more light. Believe, me you will emerge from this blackness.'

He was right. That's exactly how my life went after that. The darkness was there longer than it should have been because I was carrying a lot of issues that I wasn't even aware of. If I had received counselling or if I had known what I know now, I could have coped better.

Financially, I was luckier than many. Tom had life insurance and left me a pension. His employers, Ascon, were very good to me too, giving me Tom's company car and a large bonus at Christmas. But our baby was becoming a small boy and was growing less reliant on me. Eighteen months or so after Tom's death, he was in Montessori, and within a year, I knew he would be starting school. My baby was growing up, and I knew I needed some outlet for my own creativity, some kind of work and ideally, the type of work I could do from home.

When Tom was alive, he was well-paid and earning enough income for me to be a stay-at-home mum. But I found myself torn about being at home all the time. I found I was restless and longed to get back into the workplace. At the same time, I didn't want to be away from my baby.

'I'm not staying home all the time,' I warned Tom, 'I have to do something. I need to work too.' But I knew going back out on the road again was not an option. After some thought, I decided to use my make-up and beauty talents to set up an image and grooming course in

Ennis. I knew I could host classes on fashion, make-up and deportment. I was also a big advocate for brushes and probably the first woman in Ireland to promote the use of them. I had learnt about the use of brushes in the United States, but very few were using them in Ireland back then. I started looking around for experts in other fields of knowledge to contribute to this course.

I recruited Anne Moran, a physical education teacher and the wife of Kerry legend, Ogie Moran. She presented workshops on exercise, diet and nutrition. I also found other experts, including a good hairdresser who could consult on hairstyling. Once I had put together a great team of consultants, I created a six-week course to be held every Monday night in a room in the Old Ground Hotel in Ennis. I totted up all my expenses and realised I needed to have twenty participants to break even. After placing an advert in the local newspaper, the numbers trickled in. It was challenging to get the numbers I needed, but by the time I started the first course, I managed to find the twenty participants that I needed. Everyone was paid, and it left me with a small income for myself.

The response to the course was terrific. Everyone enjoyed it. It was very social, and everyone felt that they learnt a lot from the experience. The reaction was so positive, it encouraged me to organise the second course in image and grooming. Word of mouth from the first course did all the work for me the second time. As soon as I placed an advert in the paper, I had queues out the door for a place. I could only fit a maximum of about forty in the course, and I found myself turning people away or taking their details for the next session. I continued to do these courses on Monday nights, and then

I set up a small modelling agency in Ennis. I was only in the town for eighteen months in total, but my agency took over all the local fashion shows and promotional jobs in the area.

For me, it was ideal. I was able to look after the baby and have my own interests and business on the side. Tom took over the care of our baby on Monday nights while I presented the course. I loved what I was doing, and Tom supported me in anything I wanted to do. He was proud of the small business that I set up in Ennis.

After Tom died, I knew I needed to do something that would bring in a steady stream of income for the baby and me. Yet, it had to be something that would let me work from home and let me stay with the baby.

I hoped my devotion to Our Lady might help me to find a new direction in life, so I went to a travel agency and booked a pilgrimage to Medjugorje in Croatia. I remember walking up and down that hill in Medjugorje to the Blue Cross, praying and praying to Our Lady. I pleaded with her to intercede and send me something that would fill the void in my life.

In 1985, Medjugorje was still in its infancy as a site of pilgrimage. It was a small village with a little stone church and cobblestone streets. People gathered outside the visionaries' homes to pray when they were having their apparitions. One day, I saw one of the visionaries winding her way through the congregation outside her house. She startled me when she stopped right in front of me, smiled and took me by the hand. She led me into her small village house to bestow me with the honour of witnessing one of the daily apparitions of Our Lady. I watched the visionary enter her spiritual trance, but experienced nothing out of the ordinary in that spartanly furnished room. At the same time, I left with a vague sense of reassurance that Our Lady had heard my prayers and would help me.

After returning home, I decided it was time to seek out new business ideas for our future. I felt the place to start the search was in

America because every popular trend there migrated to Europe soon after. However, crime levels were at an all-time high in cities like New York in the eighties, so I didn't want to risk bringing my son there. Instead, I decided that I would go to Halifax in Novia Scotia in Canada, where I had a friend and which seemed a lot safer.

I started my research by combing through the shopping centres with Tom in tow. I noted the queues outside the Burger King chain, which was taking off around Canada at that time. The fast-food franchise was yet to arrive in Ireland then. I also saw queues form outside health food restaurants serving green juices, whole foods and organic foods. The health food trend appealed more to me than fast food, but I didn't feel any real passion for the restaurant business, and it didn't suit my lifestyle as a single mother.

My dream was to find something that allowed me the flexibility to work from home or to stay with my baby. I stayed with my friend, Jean, in Halifax for the first couple of days. Jean, who was always beautifully dressed, looked me up and down one day.

'Marion,' she said, 'you have such nice clothes, but your colours are all over the place.'

I didn't know what she was on about.

'My colours?'

'I think you would enjoy having your colours done. And if you're looking for business, it might be something that would work for you. It's very popular.'

It was fashion related, so I was intrigued. I made an appointment and a day or so later walked in the door of a place called Colours in Halifax. I sat down and began to learn all about the science of colour analysis. It only took a few minutes, before I thought, *thank you, Our Lady. My prayers are answered.*

I knew that I was going to love this. It married everything I loved, make-up, fashion, image and esteem. I discovered colour analysis is about helping us choose the fabric shades and make-up that enhance our skin tone, eyes and hair colour. It was like the veils dropped from my eyes, and I thought, *that's why that jacket looks so bad on me and why this scarf makes me feel so good. This all makes so much sense!*

When I was working in Brown Thomas, which was Cash's then, I often worked alongside a beautiful-looking Kerry woman. Breda had this glorious mane of chestnut hair, sallow skin and brown eyes, and she would put on an orange lipstick and look like a goddess. Everybody in the department tried on the same orange lipstick, but we looked like clowns. I couldn't figure out how she looked so well and why the same lipstick looked so awful on me. She was a person with Autumn colouring, so the orange lipstick and autumn tones were perfect for her. Now the final parts of the image consultancy puzzle were falling into place for me, and I was a complete convert. I thought, *if only I had this knowledge for the image and grooming courses I held in Ennis!*

That afternoon I went back and had my style done. Style analysis identified what worked for me, my body frame and personality. I was absolutely on a high. *This course is fantastic,* I thought. *This is exactly what I'm looking for.* I was buzzing with enthusiasm as I returned to Ireland, and my immediate plan was to introduce the Colours franchise to the country.

Mum and Dad came to Dublin to collect us at the airport. Mum sat in the back of the car so she could fuss over Tom. I was sitting in front with Dad, who was the most practical man you'd ever meet in your life. He loved business, but he was a cautious man. He had grown up in poverty and had a terrible fear of returning there. He was anxious for me to mind my money, especially as I was a widow and a single mum.

'Dad, I found a fantastic business!' I said.

I was dying to tell everyone about my incredible discovery.

'What is it, love?'

He loved anything to do with enterprise.

'I found this business where I tell people what colours they can wear to suit their complexion and to work with the hair and their eye colour.'

'What? You mean you tell them what colours they have to wear, and you think they're going to pay you for that?'

'Of course, they're going to pay me.'

'Oh, sweetheart of God, you want people to pay you to tell them what colours they should wear? I never heard such rubbish now in my life.'

He appealed to my mother in the back of the car.

'Sheila, are you listening to this? Would you ever talk some sense into her? She's going to spend all this money training in this colour thing, and she wants people to pay her to tell them what colour to wear.'

My mother was always a woman with her own mind.

'I think it sounds very interesting,' she said. 'Anyway, Marion has always been lucky in business, so leave her be. If she believes in it, it will happen.'

I remember two years later, I won my first award for the highest sales in Europe, and I waved the certificate in my dad's face.

'See Dad, I won an award for all this colours 'rubbish'!' I teased.

My astute dad didn't bat an eyelid.

'I've no interest in a piece of paper,' he sniffed. 'The only way you'll impress me is by showing me your bank balance.'

NEW LOVE

The music was pounding, the lights flashing and the only other people in the club were a group of nurses on a hen-night at the bar. I had been working late, and my girlfriend and I were enjoying late drinks, trying to catch up over the loud music.

Shortly after we sat down, two guys descended the stairs into the club. By now, I was thirty-eight, absorbed with rearing my young son and building my own small but thriving business empire. They were random young fellows, of no interest at all to me. In the ordinary course of things, they might have started chatting up the young nurses at the bar. It's still a wonder to me that somehow, I ended up marrying one of these two men.

Even though I was a young, attractive widow, my love life took a back seat for many years after Tom. My passions were my son and my rapidly growing image consultancy business. Emotionally, I wasn't in a good place for a long time. I dated, of course, and I met some nice men, but my heart wasn't in these relationships. I talked about my late husband too much for some of them. Others wanted to settle down when I just wasn't ready. The truth was, I wasn't free in my soul. Happily, I had my son and my business, both of which I loved, and poured my energy into, and they filled the void in my life for a long time.

I used money from the insurance I received from Tom's death to set myself up in the new image consultancy and colour analysis venture. My attempts to bring the Canadian franchise to Ireland proved too tricky, because it required moving to Dublin. Instead, I found a new franchise in the UK and became one of the first Irish women to train there. I converted my garage into a studio with a £10,000 investment in old Irish punts, and I paid £10,000 in pounds sterling to go to London and train in colour and image and style.

My classmates were mostly Scandinavian, a couple of French women and a few women who came from cities scattered around Britain. But there was little time for socialising or getting to know each other. The course was designed to be brief but intense and involved twelve-hour days packed into two weeks.

I took to this new field of image consultancy straight away. Having a background in cosmetics, fashion and accessories, I was in familiar territory from the start. My practical experience played a huge role in helping me understand everything.

Visually, the whole thing made sense, and everything fell into place for me. This training was the icing on the cake of everything I'd already learnt and enhanced all the knowledge that I'd acquired over the years. Everything dovetailed together beautifully. Discovering image consultancy seemed as if all the final secrets of cosmetics and fashion had been revealed to me. I felt I'd come home, and I loved the course.

Before I could start my new business, I also had to buy a start-up stock of make-up and accessories. In total, between training costs, converting the garage and buying stock, my new start-up cost me around £25,000 in Irish punts, or €31,750. I was ready to go except I didn't have any budget left for advertising or marketing.

Someone up above was looking after me because a higher power seemed to promote my fledgling business. My friend, Mary

Morgan, happened to be interviewed by Anita Hooley from the Cork Examiner the week I qualified.

'You should talk to Marion,' Mary urged. 'She's starting a new business, and it's something that will interest the women of Cork.' So, thanks to her, Anita did a profile on me and my new business.

I had also been interviewed by Moya Doherty a year earlier for an RTE TV programme called Turning Point, but it hadn't yet been broadcast. I qualified my training in London on a Friday and learnt the TV programme was about to be broadcast the following Tuesday. It was great timing because it raised my profile and other media took an interest.

I couldn't have paid for all this free publicity. I never had to advertise, and from the day I started, my phone never stopped ringing.

'Your mum is going to be a very busy woman!' I told Tom, leafing through my diary in amazement. I was booked up weeks in advance.

I was afraid that the business might trail off afterwards, but word-of-mouth did all the rest of the work for me. As soon as one nurse arrived, I'd have a hospital load of nurses booking in. The same happened with schoolteachers; as soon as one arrived, the rest of the teachers in the school followed. Events and bookings from businesswomen, businessmen, politicians and corporates flooded in too.

I made one mistake during those early years. When I came back from London, I was the only person in Cork providing colour and style consultancy. But I often mentioned the franchise name and the brand I worked under. Unwittingly, I was promoting the franchise and the brand.

The recommendation I would give anybody now is that you promote yourself in business, not someone else's brand or franchise. Essentially, I let the brand cash in on my hard work in marketing. Others went and trained with the franchise as a result, so I could have hurt my business. I continued to work very profitably in image consultancy and makeovers, but it took a while to realise that my own name is my biggest business asset and an essential part of my brand. Any of us may move on from someone else's brand or a franchise, but our name stays with us. It was just another learning experience.

My new business was the ideal job for a single mum. Everything revolved around Tom. I was able to work in the mornings when my little boy was in nursery school, and my afternoons were devoted to him. After he went to bed, I called in a babysitter, so I could host evening presentations and consults.

All through this time, I worked hard, and I loved it, but I was still struggling emotionally. In Ireland of the eighties, I didn't go for counselling, and I certainly didn't take medication. My family and friends were a great support, but they were not professionals in counselling and healing. It took me years to realise how important it is to be able to talk to somebody who is professionally trained, who can see the bigger picture and who sees our familiar landscapes from a different perspective.

So, I was blessed to find a business that I loved. My company gave me a passion for life and a devotion to something else other than rearing my child. Within a couple of years of starting, the franchise honoured me at one of their big annual conventions in the UK as the company's Best International Consultant. It was also good for me because it transformed me into something more than Tom Creedon's widow. There was a Tom Creedon Cup and even a poem in memory of Tom Creedon. Tom Creedon Park came later. But by having my own business, I felt I rediscovered my own unique and separate identity. God love me, I thought I was my business for a long time. I was good at it, and I loved it, so that was how I wanted to be seen. I didn't realise for a long time that I was much more than the business I remained in for thirty years.

Being in business filled the loneliness of being on my own at home. It meant that I was meeting new people every day and working a few nights a week. It was my salvation because I felt useful and productive and enjoyed feeling that I was helping others to bring out the best of themselves.

For a long time, I thought I was destined to be on my own the rest of my life. I was a single woman raising a child, and I had to make sure to provide for both of us. My priority in business was to provide for Tom and myself and to shore up my future by becoming financially independent

I think I must have inherited some of my business acumen from my father, who was always shrewd with money. I decided to look after my future by investing in property from very early on. Using the remainder of Tom's insurance money as deposits, I applied for mortgages from the bank and bought an apartment and a commercial building. It was a struggle to begin with, but I knew they would provide a good pension in later life.

Meanwhile, my business was round-the-clock busy with endless consultations and presentations. Also, because I worked from home, people felt they could drop in for a free consultation anytime, often at night.

'I was with you a few weeks ago, and I was just passing, so I thought I'd drop in to show you this sweater – it's not exactly the right shade but do you think it's close enough or should I bring it back?' they would say.

Or else they would call on a Sunday afternoon brandishing an empty lipstick from their make-up bags.

'Marion, I was just passing, and I need this lipstick,' they'd say.

 Again, it was my fault because I didn't set boundaries. I could have said 'no', but they were at my door, so I'd say, 'Oh sure, come in.' Clients monopolised my child's time sometimes, but I didn't know any better. I was always trying to look after the client when I would have been better looking after myself first. The client is paying, of course, but they are only paying for a certain amount of my time. That was something that I also had to learn later.

I did yearn for the kind of love and intimacy that I had shared with Tom, but no one came close to filling the void that his death left in my life. I wasn't in that space where I could find love because I wasn't willing to let go of Tom. In my head, I still felt married to him, and there was a sense of guilt about meeting other men.

'I wonder if we'll ever meet anyone that we will want to live with again,' I remember saying to my friend Helen Casey, who was also a young widow. Her husband, a hurler, died the year before Tom, and she had a son so we had shared experiences.

At one stage, we both went to see the White Witch of Cobh, who was a well-known fortune teller. 'There's good news here,' the White Witch said, reading my palm. 'You're going to be really successful in your business.'

Okay, I thought, *that's good news, but is that it?* It wasn't. She looked a bit harder and she saw a man in my future.

'I see a very tall and handsome guy, who will travel by boat to see you and will be very important in your life!'

That cheered me up. I told Helen afterwards, 'I'm going to meet a guy who will arrive on his yacht into Kinsale and sweep me off my feet!'

The White Witch told Helen that she was going to meet a wonderful man in a white coat, who would be in her life for many, many years.

'I'm going to marry a rich doctor!' said Helen, equally delighted with her fortune.

However, my man on the yacht in Kinsale didn't appear in the weeks or months afterwards, and dating was a struggle. A lot of the time, it felt easier to avoid the complications of dating.

A few times, I met lovely men, but the right one didn't come along for nine years after I lost Tom.

It happened one night when I arranged a babysitter and met Marian in town. It was after work, so it was late on a Tuesday night when we met. We went to a club for a late drink, and as expected, the club was quiet apart from a few nurses who were on a hen night. The place was so empty that we couldn't miss the sight of two young guys arriving into the club. One of them was strikingly tall and good looking. Marian was great fun, but she was a mischief-maker. She had a husband at home, but she liked to play matchmaker with me, and I could see her eyeing up this poor guy.

I shot her a warning look. 'Please Marian,' I said. 'Don't start. Don't draw anyone on me. I have no interest. Let's just enjoy a few drinks.' But she couldn't resist. At some stage, she went up to the tall young guy, and I raised my eyes to heaven as she led him to me. He was handsome and charming, and I was polite, but I wasn't encouraging.

At the end of the night, we all parted ways, and that might have been the end of it. But destiny brought me and the handsome man together again.

A month or so later, I went out again with my cousin. We were in the same nightclub when a fellow with chiselled good looks approached me. He was smiling at me as if he recognised me, and he looked vaguely familiar. *Who's this fellow again?* I thought, my mind racing. I had a notion that he must be the guard who had stopped me recently for my insurance. It took me a minute to realise that he was the guy Marian had accosted on my behalf weeks earlier.

His name was Cormac Hegarty, and we talked for a while, but when I realised he was thirty years old - a full eight years younger than me - I lost interest. *This isn't going to go anywhere,* I thought. *He's too young, and we have nothing in common.* But Cormac wasn't easily deterred.

'I'd really like to go out with you,' he said.

In the end, I said, 'Look, my phone number is in the book. Call me if you want to.'

I didn't expect to hear from him again, but he did ring me at home one evening. I made some excuse not to meet him. 'Yes, sure, give me a call another time.'

He did ring again and again. He was from Curraheen in Cork and was travelling over and back from England where he was working in property development and construction.

When he told me that he was travelling from the UK by boat, I remembered the words of the White Witch of Cobh. Needless to say, the man who was sailing his yacht into Kinsale to meet me never materialised.

Incidentally, Helen *did* also meet the man in a white coat as foretold by the White Witch, and she's been in a happy relationship with a butcher for the last twenty years!

Cormac was still living in London when I met him, but he was planning to return to Ireland for good. His brother Diarmuid had died tragically, and he wanted to be home as a support for his parents. Diarmuid's death had shocked Cormac and affected him badly. It probably made him more understanding of me and my ambivalence about dating him. Finally, he said, 'I'm going to give you my number, and when you're ready to go out, you ring me.'

Weeks later, my cousin was invited on a blind date in Kinsale. 'I'm not going unless you come with me!' she said. 'Find someone, anyone and come with me!' I thought, *where am I going to get someone to go with me?* And then I remembered that handsome young guy from London and Curraheen.

So, our first official date was part of a foursome with my cousin in Kinsale. I thought it would be a bit of fun, a night out. I didn't have any expectations apart from a few drinks and a bit of diversionary entertainment watching my cousin with her blind date.

I knew by then that Cormac didn't talk much. He was quiet and polite, and he had a lovely, warm smile that made his eyes crinkle attractively. *It's such a shame that there's such an age difference,* I thought.

It was a long time afterwards that I learnt that Cormac's abiding memory of that date was one of pure terror. I volunteered to drive to Kinsale that evening. The roads in the area are quite narrow, but I know them like the back of my hand. So, I chatted away all the way to Kinsale swinging down and around the country roads, driving as usual on the upper edge of the speed limits. I was oblivious to Cormac gripping the dashboard and slamming his foot on imaginary brakes.

Cormac remembers our date as a white-knuckle ride careering down the country roads. *This one thinks she's a rally driver,* he thought, bracing himself, convinced we'd end up in a ditch. He said he was never so grateful to get out of a car when we reached Kinsale. But then his next thought was *Oh Jesus, I have to travel home with her again.*

Of course, I didn't know anything about Cormac suffering a near-death experience on that date for a long time, because he never said anything. He was definitely the dark and silent type. I realise now that Cormac, like my husband before him, is the type of man I'm attracted to because they remind me of my father, another quiet, refined and gentle man. It's only taken me about forty years to realise the pattern.

Back then, I just thought Cormac was a lovely man, a gentleman who listened, smiled easily, but was reserved too. I also felt he was very secure for a young guy, relaxed and comfortable in his skin. However, he had one additional flaw on top of the age difference.

'I met this nice guy,' I told Helen. 'But he's the worst dressed man I ever met!' And he was. He wore the same old trench coat and shabby T-shirts all the time. He had no interest in clothes. I took him to meet Helen in Jury's Hotel in Cork one evening.

'Now, you listen to me!' she said afterwards. 'He's the nicest guy I've ever met with you. If you don't like what he's wearing, find him something that you do like, but in the meantime, get over yourself!' She was right, of course, and I already was beginning to realise that this man had a big heart and a beautiful soul.

He was also divine to look at; six foot three, lean and athletic, with a runner's physique, and he was intelligent and interesting to talk to. I admired him, and I liked his confidence and independence. He didn't follow the crowd, and he wasn't one of those young guys who had to be in the pub with the lads every weekend. I discovered he loved business, so we were like-minded souls in that regard.

But I was resistant to the relationship partly because of the age difference. It didn't bother Cormac, but it made a difference to me. To be honest, I hid him from most my friends in the beginning of our relationship. I'd meet him outside of town and in places where I knew I wouldn't meet people I knew. My mother's response upon meeting Cormac didn't help matters. 'He's a lovely guy alright,' she said. 'He'd be perfect for June,' referring to my sister who is sixteen years younger than me.

I felt a lot of conflict about him being younger. On the one hand, I doubted that he would be invested in the relationship. I felt he wouldn't commit, and he would move on. On the other hand, I was worried that he would commit, and he would eventually desire a family. I didn't know if it could ever happen with me.

My boy was also a significant stumbling block in my relationship with Cormac. Tom's life was a stable one, and I didn't want him getting attached to someone who might not be around in a few months. Tom and I were comfortable, and we had our routine. I suppose we were living in a comfortable rut. I was afraid a man in my life might upset our cosy little world. Of course, my child had his own life and was involved in tennis, swimming and rugby. But I was the one who drove him here, there and everywhere. His school was on the far side of the city, so between Tom and my business, my life was full too.

There was a bit of defiance also because I felt like I didn't need anyone. I'd made a comfortable life for myself, and I was financially secure on my own. I think there was a lot of fear, also. My husband Tom was with me one minute and was gone the next. I didn't really understand it at the time, but a fear of abandonment haunted me after Tom's death. In my subconscious, there was that terror if I opened my heart again, I could end up being hurt. Fear of abandonment was huge.

Yet, there was a loneliness in my life. I felt an emptiness in the emotional sense of not having a partner. I wanted a partner, and then I didn't. I just felt a lot of insecurity about the relationship, and I didn't know what I wanted. In my head, there were too many obstacles to us becoming serious. Cormac and I had an on-again, off-again relationship for a long time.

As the months rolled on, my resistance to the relationship began to make less and less sense. I could see that Cormac was serious about me and our relationship. He was lovely to Tom, and my boy was mad about him. I met his family and really liked them. His mother was from Booterstown in Dublin, and his father, from Lough Hyne in West Cork. They were good people, and they were welcoming and generous as parents considering that I was a widow with a child and eight years older than their son. But it was probably a year before I relaxed and became more committed to our relationship.

We were a couple for about eighteen months when I discovered I was pregnant. Cormac was elated. We were in a whirl of excitement; both of us ecstatic about the prospect of a baby. I always wanted another baby, but I didn't want to have a baby alone. I didn't have any doubts that Cormac would be a devoted dad. Yet, marriage wasn't something I even thought of before this, but when Cormac asked me to marry him, it all seemed so perfect.

A new baby, a new husband, a chance for a new life. I never dreamt that I could find so much happiness a second time. I realised that I wanted nothing more in the world than to marry Cormac, so I didn't hesitate. I said 'yes!'

THE WEDDING

*a*s I passed Tom's bedroom door, I thought I heard something, and I stopped in shock. *Is that my boy crying in there?* I thought, listening at the door. Tom had learnt that day that Cormac and I were getting married. His response had been much as I expected: surprise, happiness, excitement about being part of the wedding and, after a while, a side order of not really caring that much. As a ten-year-old boy, he had lots of distractions like swimming and friends and could only be expected to show an interest in the dull affairs of adults for so long.

Me and Cormac on our wedding day 20 April, 1992.

'You'll be able to invite all your friends to the party, and you know that you have to give me away at the church?' I told him.

Tom was delighted that he would have a starring role at the wedding. My father had died the year before, which was a cruel blow to Tom because he and his grandfather were remarkably close. Dad was only sixty-five when he was diagnosed with stomach cancer and was given three months to live. I was devastated by the news, and all my fears of abandonment kicked in again. It was heart-breaking to hear my father say one of his greatest regrets was that he couldn't live to see Tom grow up to be the fine young man he knew he'd become. My dad had been a wonderful presence in Tom and my life. For his last months, I struggled thinking 'how am I going to cope without this wonderful man in our lives?'

Cormac's dad, John Hegarty, my mum Sheila, me and
Cormac, his mother Maureen and my brother, Sean Goggin
at our wedding 20 April, 1992.

But I learnt that the fear of abandonment is far worse than abandonment itself. In the end, of course, both Tom and I managed without him. It was Dad's time to go, and he had a full life and was loved. Our lives went on, and now Tom and I had Cormac. This man loved both of us and was committing to be a permanent part of our lives. To me, it seemed like my father had sent him to us. I hadn't anticipated that Tom would react badly to us getting married.

I knew a new baby might complicate things, but Cormac and I decided to cross that bridge later. We told no one about the baby, agreeing that it was our journey for the time being. The pregnancy would become self-evident in time, but in the meanwhile, it was something beautiful and private between us.

The last thing I expected was my boy would be unhappy. Yet, here he was sobbing to himself in his room. *Maybe this is all going too fast for all of us,* I worried.

I went into the bedroom, and I could see his face was tear-streaked and his expression anguished. The sight broke my heart.

'What's wrong, darling?' I said. 'Why are you crying? It's not about Cormac and I getting married, is it?'

He nodded forlornly, and all the joy I had been feeling seemed to plummet somewhere into my boots.

'I don't see why you have to get married, Mummy. Aren't we just grand the way we are?'

My stomach lurched. I didn't expect this reaction at all.

'Why don't you want me to marry Cormac? I thought you really liked him?'

He sighed.

'Because you're going to be Hegarty, and I'm going to be Creedon and the boys in school will laugh at me because my mum has a different name to me.'

I knew I could put an end to that worry.

'Look, if that's all that's worrying you, I'll keep your name,' I said. I hadn't even thought of it before, but that's when I decided to become Marion Creedon Hegarty; The 'Creedon' part is for my son, and the 'Hegarty' is for my husband.

'Are you happy with that? Would you like that?'

He seemed mollified, but still, he shrugged, and his lower lip quivered. He was a smart kid and was trying to work out what other leverage he could gain because of this wedding.

'You still don't want me to get married? Then you have to make a deal with me, Tom. Okay?'

He was startled. He never expected the wedding to be up for negotiation, but I knew my child.

'When you're a bit older and when all your friends are going to nightclubs and football marches and going out with girls, will you promise to stay in and mind me? If you promise to stay in and mind me, then I won't get married.'

Honest to God, the child didn't hesitate for an instant.

'Alright so, Mummy, you can get married.'

That was the end of Tom's angst over the wedding. Next, I visited my late husband's mum, Majella, to tell her that Cormac and I were getting married.

'I didn't think you'd ever remarry, Marion,' she said. 'But Cormac's a very nice guy and a good guy. I know he'll look after Tom.'

We both knew that Cormac would make a good stepdad, and he is a great stepdad. I made an excellent choice for Tom and me.

We had a small wedding with just a few friends and our families on 20 April 1992. It was Easter Monday, and we got married in Grange Church where I was living. The wedding was a casual affair, so I wore a hat and a soft white dress with a tea-length skirt and a fitted jacket, which I had bought in Brown Thomas.

We had a lovely day. It was small, fun and intimate, and Cormac and I were very happy. But we had no idea that our happiness was going to be so short-lived.

My first scan took place shortly after the wedding. I was just over three months pregnant when I went to the Bon Secours Maternity Hospital full of happiness and anticipation. I was also feeling great apart from the bouts of morning sickness.

The obstetrician carried out the ultrasound scan and left the room, and then he came in again and scanned again and went out again. This happened on a number of occasions.

God, he's thorough, but am I ever going to get out of here? I wondered. Then he came in with a nurse. Then they both looked solemn as they scanned and scanned again, and still it never clicked with me. Then he said the words, 'There's no heartbeat.'

My pulse started to race, and a wave of nausea rose in my throat.

'What do you mean?' I managed to stammer.

'We can't find a heartbeat, any movement,' he said, and he and the nurse gazed at me sadly, sympathetically, willing me to understand.

There's no heartbeat. My dream world, a world filled with thoughts of Cormac and me cradling our baby and Tom playing with his new brother or sister, was shattered in an instant. The much-wanted baby that we already loved was dead. I crumpled there and then. I sobbed, pleaded, begged for them to be wrong, to check again, to do something, anything.

I tried to call Cormac at work, but I couldn't reach him. My sister Celine and her husband Billy came to pick up my pieces instead that day. I remember Billy shaking his head and saying, 'There's some crow did a lump on you, girl.'

Cormac arrived home that evening oblivious to everything that had gone on. By then I was just a mass of pain and heartache, and there was no preamble. 'The baby's dead,' I said, and I remember the expression on his face because it was as if somebody shot him.

We struggled after that as a couple because I withdrew into myself; I was very depressed. I went on the fertility drug, Clomid, then for months and the weight piled on with bloating and water retention associated with the medication. I was forty by now, and my confidence was rock bottom. Meanwhile, Cormac was a very handsome man of thirty-two, and I felt even more insecure. After six months, when I still hadn't become pregnant, the doctor suggested that we try In Vitro Fertilisation or IVF. My hopes were raised again. So, we did all the tests and made an appointment for a consultation in a fertility clinic in Dublin.

We made a big deal of the consultation, staying overnight in a lovely hotel. I also made a hair appointment with the renowned David Marshall salon in Dawson Street. I was sure things would turn around. The IVF would make my dream of a baby with Cormac come true, and I would celebrate by having my hair done in the premier hair salon in the country. It was going to be all right. We were sure of it.

We went to the clinic full of optimism to meet with the fertility specialist, a Scottish man. We were brought into his surgery, where he leafed through a file of our results, and then he dropped the bombshell.

'I'm very sorry, but we can't do IVF,' he said. 'Cormac, your results are perfect but Marion, there's a hormonal problem here. You're not a suitable candidate for IVF.' There was more, but I didn't really hear anything else. My dream of a baby was crushed. I was devastated and inconsolable, and Cormac was so upset for me.

'Marion, this doesn't matter. We have Tom; we have our family, and we don't need anyone else,' he said this over and over again. He was a rock, but I couldn't be consoled that day. The flood gates opened, and the tears wouldn't stop pouring. I was grieving this huge loss of a child that I'd never have.

I still went to David Marshall's, of course. I had no interest in getting my hair done, to be honest, but I didn't feel I could cancel an appointment at the last minute. I think I was on autopilot. The stylist looking after me was from Cork and couldn't have been sweeter, but I cried all through the appointment. I managed to explain away my tears by telling him that someone belonging to me had died, but I could hardly talk, I was sobbing so much. Poor Cormac was hovering outside, peering in the window and coming in every ten minutes to check on me.

'Are you alright, Marion? Are you sure you're alright? I'll get you out of here if you want to go.' He was so caring and supportive, even though he must have been as disappointed and as upset as I was.

Afterwards, I remember thinking of my adopted cousins, who I've always adored. We were all reared with the word 'adopted', so it was always just a word. They were as much a part of the family as my other cousins. I felt Cormac and I had a lot of love to give and had so much to share, and I thought of the joy a small baby or child would bring to our house. But Cormac seemed indifferent to the idea of adoption. 'I don't think it's something I want,' he said, simply.

I brought home some of the leaflets and paperwork about the adoption process anyway and left them on the hall table. A week later, he still hadn't picked them up, so I swept them away and didn't say any more about it after that.

That winter seemed darker than most winters before. It was a very traumatic time for us both, and I plunged into a terrible depression. I remember lying on the couch, and the sense of despair was so deep that taking a shower or brushing my teeth was beyond me some days. There was no colour left in the world again, only bottomless pain.

The miscarriage brought everything back like a vast wave of pain from the past again. I was drowning in a sense of hopelessness. It was awful. I didn't even know if I wanted to be married anymore. I thought, *what is the point of anything, anymore?* Cormac did his best, but even his love and support couldn't bring me back.

My good friend, Mary Groeger, an occupational therapist and a counsellor who works in mental health, called to see me one day, and she saw me prostrate and listless on the couch. I felt spent, sick, lifeless; I didn't care if I lived or died.

'I think you need to see someone, Marion,' she said.

Despair and pain weren't new to me. I had attended all sorts of weekend workshops and joined bereavement groups after Tom died, but never found much relief. This time, however, Mary arranged for me to see a psychiatrist and experience one-to-one therapy for the first time. My only regret is that it took me over a decade to seek proper treatment and counselling.

This was my first step into self-care and into a space that was all my own. It was a place where I could explore the painful events I experienced. I found it hugely helpful. I struggled through the worst times in my life without counselling, and now, I'll go for therapy if I break a fingernail. The psychiatrist prescribed an anti-depressant, the first time I had ever taken medication to cope.

'See how you feel in a few weeks,' she said. 'I think you will find that it helps.'

I took the anti-depressants gratefully. I was glad to try anything that would lift me from the dark well I was trapped in. The combination of professional therapy and medication helped considerably, and my dark mood began to lift. I was able to start bringing down the doses of anti-depressant and then come off them entirely. I would take the medication again if I found myself going through another challenging time. For me, it's comforting to have this safety net. I know it's something that I can use to improve how I feel, but I prefer to do without it.

Therapy has also helped me to accept that it is okay to have days when we feel low. We all have these days. Before this time, I used to wonder what was wrong with me. I interpreted my low mood as a form of personal failure. Now I sit with it, try to figure out the source of the problem, and I'm gentle with myself. I don't beat myself up because I sometimes happen to feel below par.

Our hopes for another child didn't work out, but I'm glad that we tried to go for IVF because I might have always wondered, 'what if?' Cormac has never, ever in all the years raised the fact we never had a child together as an issue. He loves Tom and always says, 'We've more than enough with the one anyway.' In hindsight, I think I was the one who wanted another child but had to accept that it wasn't going to happen. That's life, and it's all fine now.

I feel so blessed to find great love in my life a second time. Cormac and I are so close - best friends in life, and great partners in business. He helped turn around my business from early on. I remember we were home one Sunday morning, and he was going through the prices that I was paying for cosmetics and for the fabric colour swatches that I gave to my clients.

'Marion, you buy so much stuff, and you make very little out of it,' he said.

I knew it was true. There was only a tiny margin on all the cosmetics, accessories and swatches that I sold.

'Why are you doing this?' he asked. 'Why can't you start your own brand and make your own products?'

It was one of those lightbulb moments. We put our heads together, and I found a manufacturer and started to get the colour swatches made for me. Then I created a cosmetics line called Top Image with a company in Germany. Making those changes turned things around and considerably raised the profit margins in my business.

Cormac and me in West Cork.

Because I worked from home, people felt entitled to show up at the door or phone me round the clock, seven days a week. It was too intrusive, and I wanted a real home life with my new husband and son. I decided to move out of the garage and get a shop in the city centre. I opened a shop called Marion Creedon Hegarty in Merchant Quay Shopping Centre. However, the rent and the overheads were high and ate into the profits. When a friend mentioned that his parents were retiring and trying to sell a building on Grand Parade, one of the main streets in Cork, I jumped at the chance. They were struggling to sell in the middle of a recession, and I was tired of shelling out dead money on rent.

'I'll buy it!' I said.

Cormac and I went to look at it. The four-storey terraced old building had subsidence and all sorts of problems, but we could see it had potential. Being a builder, Cormac was able to take over the entire project. He converted the ground floor into a shop for me and transformed the storeys upstairs into six apartments. We poured a lot of money into it, but it has been a great investment. The six apartments have never been vacant to this day. I worked for many years from the Grand Parade remises, but the ground floor is rented out to another business now.

They were busy years, as we both expanded our businesses. I became the first woman in Ireland to manufacturer a tanning range when I started Top Image Tan twenty-five years ago.

I always wore instant false tans, wash-off products that invariably streaked and were time-consuming to apply. Most tans on the market were hit-or-miss and mostly 'miss' because the shades didn't suit Irish skins. Then I received a product in the post from a manufacturer in America, and I tried it out by applying it on a friend. She came back the next day asking in wonderment, 'What is this stuff? I can't wash it off!'

I looked over her sun-kissed, streak-free tan, and it felt like I'd won the lotto.

'You can't it wash off? Oh my God, that's fantastic!'

Rather than importing it from America, I decided to see if I could manufacture this formula in Ireland or Europe. Nobody could make it in Ireland at the time, so I had to go to Europe. I put a huge amount of time and research into the range, but to this day, Top Image tan is a beautiful product.

It contains a no-streak coloured tint, so you can see where it's applied. There is no fake tan odour, and most importantly, it doesn't

come off on clothes. I spend too much on my clothes to have them ruined by fake tan.

I designed the colour specifically for pale Irish complexions, so there are no hues of copper or orange. When I launched my tanning products range, there were only two gradual tans on the Irish market - my brand and Bronze Express from France. The texture of mine was similar to the French product, but my colour was more suited to the Irish skin and lasted longer.

I did the marketing myself, mostly by giving out samples, and thankfully, the product spoke for itself. When I started Top Image Tan in the mid-nineties, my son was a teenager, so I gifted the tan to all the fifth and six-year students he knew. They passed it on to their girlfriends and their mothers, and anyone who tried it always came back as a customer.

Ideally, what I could have done is brought in a partner to market the range, but I'm not a good business partner. Like all entrepreneurs, I feel nobody can do anything as well as I can. Then United Drug discovered my product and approached me to come on board as distributors, so every major pharmacy store and beauty salon in Ireland stocked it. It's a great product that is still selling for me today despite the huge competition in the tan market today.

Cormac's grandmother came from the peaceful West Cork island, Reengaroga. We fell in love with the wild and rugged scenery, and we loved to breathe in the sea air and walk the narrow country roads at weekends. After we were married a year, we bought a site next door to where his grandmother was born. We built a house there on the hillside with panoramic views of the island, Roaring-water Bay and the Atlantic Ocean, and we used it for years as our weekend refuge and hideaway.

Me and my son, Tom outside Bushes Bar in Baltimore.

We also sold our first house in Grange Erin and built a beautiful riverbank home with an estuary view in Rochestown in 2004. Meanwhile, our son Tom moved out of home and went to UCC to study Arts. After that, he went to Dublin to study for a post-graduate degree in the Michael Smurfit Graduate Business School.

After Tom left home, Cormac and I were able to do a lot more travelling. We attended more trade fairs and got involved in more business deals. During the boom years in Ireland, we developed a derelict post office building on the bridge in Bandon and made a huge profit. I made a million euros on that property deal alone.

Cormac and me at the Fastnet lighthouse, Cork.

As well as the retail shop, I decided to go into wholesale cosmetics and accessories as well. We bought a big warehouse unit in Fashion City in Ballymount in Dublin and set up a wholesale cash and carry business. I filled the five thousand square feet full of fashion accessories for weddings, debs, casual and business wear. The stock included headpieces, scarves, earrings, bags and jewellery and all my Top Image tans and cosmetics. It did extremely well, and the Top Image brand was soon on sale in five hundred outlets. I paid off the cost of the unit within five years.

We travelled abroad a lot to stock the wholesale unit. When Tom finished in the Smurfit Business School, he became a stockbroker in Hong Kong. So, Cormac and I were travelling back and forth to see him as well.

At the same time, I never stopped doing my makeovers. I loved doing the colour and style consultancies in the shop in Cork. I tried to employ other people to expand that part of the business. However, it's a personal service industry, and people didn't want anybody except the name over the door.

My husband was busy too buying warehouses and working on building projects. While juggling his business interests, he went back to UCC and did a master's degree in business. Now he's thinking of going back again to do a PhD. His talents lie in the financial side of things, controlling costs, holding onto the reins and telling me, 'you can't spend any more!' My skills lie in selling and in bringing passion, energy and ideas to a project, so we make a good team in business.

Me with Cormac.

On the property side of things, I own a number of apartments and two commercial premises which provide my pension, but it was a team effort between Cormac and me. We don't have hobbies like tennis or golf, so the business has always been a passion shared between us. We're best friends, teammates, and I really like Cormac as a person apart from loving him as my husband. He's a wonderful man to have in my life. The best and most succinct way I can describe the relationship between Cormac and me is that we're a team; a great one.

Over the last ten years, I've developed breathing problems with COPD or Chronic obstructive pulmonary disease. It has been life-changing to manage it properly. I need to look after myself more. I must stay active, walk more and relax more.

After being hospitalised one winter, I wondered if there were treatments in America or elsewhere that would improve my condition.

'If I was your mother, what would you tell me to do?' I asked a young doctor.

'I'd have my mother on a plane out of this country around October, and I wouldn't bring her back until March,' he said. 'You have level four of COPD. Your lungs need a place which is warm and dry, and not the damp conditions we have here.'

A week later, I was out of the hospital and on my way to Playa Blanca in Lanzarote where I stayed for two months. The doctor was right because I did see a great improvement. I had difficulty walking to the bathroom at home at one stage, and now I walk four miles every day at home. I continue to spend a couple of months in Lanzarote each year to escape the worst of the Irish winter.

We sold our house in Rochestown three years ago and moved permanently to Reenaroga Island. To me, it is the most beautiful place in the world. I love the tranquil country roads which lead to the water's edge, the small empty beaches with views of the islands and the crashing waves of the Atlantic around us.

Cormac and me at Sherkin Island, West Cork.

This is supposedly our retirement, but if you saw the list of things I had to do this morning, it didn't resemble anything like a restful retreat from work. We're redesigning and recalibrating our lives into something new and different. Retirement is less like the end of the road for both of us, and more like the start of a new journey on a highspeed motorway.

There are still times when I feel my late husband in our lives. I remember a day last September when I was driving and thinking about my son and wondering if he'd get a business deal he was hoping for. I knew it would mean a lot to Tom. And then the beautiful lyrics and melody of Neil Diamond's song September Morn came on the radio. Suddenly, I was filled with this magnificent, warm feeling, a wave of comfort. September is a month which holds a lot of memories for me. It's my late husband's birthday, our wedding anniversary and our son's birthday.

Me outside my shop in Cork

And here was Neil Diamond's song filling the car, and I experienced a wonderful sense of love and joy. I knew that everything was going to be okay. It was like Tom's spirit reassuring me that he is still looking after us, and I knew that my son's dream was about to be fulfilled.

And sure enough, I got the phone call from my son to say that the deal he had waited on for months had gone through. It had happened just as I felt it would after hearing the song. Well, that's my take on what happened that morning, and that works for me, so I'm owning it.

I played September Morn for Cormac afterwards, telling him about the sensation that I felt. It really feels like Tom is looking after us all of us as a family, Cormac, Tom and me. Cormac never ever objects to me talking or remembering Tom. He has always also been respectful of my needs around my late husband's memory. He accepts it as part of me, part of the package of who I am and part of our son, Tom, but knows it is something in the past, separate from our life and our family.

The shadow of the late Tom Creedon might have been too much for some men but not for Cormac. Somebody once asked him, 'How do you cope with this Tom Creedon legend thing?' Cormac just shrugged.

'I'm far more worried about the live fellows than I am about a dead one,' he said.

He knows that I'm the woman I am today because of pain, suffering and loss and all that I went through in the past. Cormac has been through his own loss and pain too, so he understands.

He has never appeared to be threatened by the past, nor should he. He is just a really good man, kind and caring, and we adore each other. That's a lovely feeling to have, and we regularly say how blessed we feel to have found each other.

I never take what we have for granted. Because of my history, I'm more conscious than most that there might not be a tomorrow. So, I'm very aware of living in the moment, enjoying the 'now' with Cormac, truly appreciating it and cherishing our wonderful lives together.

Me and Cormac at a friend's wedding.

PART II
THE MIND MAKEOVER

MARION THE MENTOR

*L*ike most people, I spent many years rushing along life's treadmill. My days were filled with raising my son and running my business. I was preoccupied with providing for us and paying the bills and keeping my head above water. Grief, anxiety and abandonment remained as issues in my life during those years. I suffered from depression and loneliness at times. I drank too much, and I often didn't feel like I had control over my own behaviour and feelings.

When I fell into a deep depression after the miscarriage of Cormac's and my baby in 1992, I sought professional counselling for the first time. Being in therapy for the first time brought me more in touch with my feelings. I began to understand my thoughts and behaviours better, and my self-awareness began to grow.

When my son Tom moved out at age eighteen and went off to college, I was hit by a bad bout of empty nest syndrome. Oh, I cried buckets! I struggled after he left, and I felt terribly depressed and lonely. One day, I happened to be shopping in Marks and Spencer's store in Cork, and I bumped into a friend, Clare.

'I've just finished a Social and Health course with the Southern Health Board,' she said. 'Do you know what, Marion, I think you'd be great for it!'

She said, *'you'd be great for it.'* Now, if Clare had said the course would be *good for me*, I probably wouldn't have heard her. She just happened to phrase it in a way that I would be great for the course. It was providence because, at that point, I wanted to feel needed and so, what she said grabbed my attention. I thought this course might be something that I could contribute to or lead to something I could contribute to. When Clare said she'd enquire if there were any places left on the next course, I didn't brush her off as I might have.

I'm so happy that I met Clare that day. This course became a big step in my journey to self-discovery and personal development. The year-long programme in personal and community empowerment was life-transforming for me. I had trained in image, fashion and make-up, which I loved, but this course nourished my spiritual and emotional side. It gave me greater insight into myself and the people around me.

But I was still looking for peace, looking for answers and more understanding, more acceptance. I didn't know exactly what I was looking for, but I knew there was something I needed. I went for counselling to clinical psychologist, Doctor Tony Humphreys and found him to be a brilliant man with a beautiful and perceptive soul. Therapy with Tony greatly helped, but then he suggested something that prompted another big step in self-discovery.

'Marion, would you think about studying interpersonal communications in University College Cork?' he said, one day.

I was reluctant because I didn't feel I was capable of third-level education. I didn't have the confidence to tackle a university course.

'It could be a wonderful journey for you,' he said. 'Think about it. I would highly recommend it.'

I told him I would think about it, and I came home that night and read the programme. Interpersonal Communications offered students the opportunity to examine their lives and develop their potential. The prospectus said that participants would become skilled in effective listening and communicating with the self and others. At that stage, I was doing workshops on personal development and spirituality nearly every weekend anyway, so I thought, *what am I afraid of? This is the journey I'm already on.*

So, that's how I ended up spending the next two years studying Interpersonal Communications, finishing up in 2005. I enjoyed every moment of my time in college. My eyes were opened. I learnt so much again about love and compassion for myself and others.

Then I met someone from my class who went on to complete a level eight honours degree course in Relationship Mentoring. She told me it was a tough course in terms of exams and papers, but she was ecstatic about it. The last two courses that I had completed were life-enhancing experiences, so her enthusiasm made me decide to give this a go too. This programme was rooted in the theories and practices of psychoanalysis, psychotherapy, sociological theories and experimental psychology.

I felt intimidated in the beginning because there were only three or four of us on the course who hadn't already been awarded a level seven degree. Yet, I persevered and managed to qualify as a relationship mentor after two years in UCC. I also received my first ever 'A' grade on that course, and I nearly wore it on my forehead, I was so proud. I met the most fabulous men and women on this journey, and several of us continue to hold a workshop every month.

Me, the graduate, with husband Cormac and son, Tom.

Each step of this journey of learning has been transformative. This education has given me better control of my life and my emotions, and I've learnt to create positive changes that I had been aching for.

I no longer feel overwhelmed by difficult emotions, and I have the techniques and tools to decrease stress and anxiety. I have gained greater clarity about who I am, what I'm capable of and what I need to do to look after myself.

I rarely experience depression anymore, and when I do, I know how to handle it. Increased self-knowledge has helped me to review and assess the thoughts, actions, feelings, and conversations that I have with other people. It has helped me become more accepting of myself and others.

Because I can be more authentic and express my emotions more freely and clearly, I'm able to form deeper attachments with people. I also make sure to surround myself with people who enhance my life rather than detract from it. For me, education has helped achieve greater self-awareness, increased my self-confidence and has allowed me to make positive changes.

In the following pages, I'd like to share some of the insights, the knowledge and tools that have dramatically improved my well-being and are helping me to live the best life that I can. My sincere hope is that something may resonate with you and help you too.

WHAT ARISES IN ME IS ABOUT ME

I recall a time a few years ago when I was sitting at a table with a group of women, friends and acquaintances over lunch. It was a light, fun get-together and then one woman leaned in from across the table and said, 'Marion, do you remember back when you were lovely and thin?'

Now, the younger Marion would have either gone into defensive mode saying, 'How dare you!' or she would have gone into attack mode by sneering, 'Is this the kettle calling the pot black?'

Either way, the whole afternoon would have been ruined in an exchange of unkind and negative jibes. That Marion would have been devastated. The comment would have gone around in her head for days like a carousel, and she would have bristled with fury. She would have worried that she looked fat or if she had worn the wrong thing.

The newer me didn't get worked up about it. Instead, I was able to respond to the woman's jibe with a bright smile and continue my conversation with the women around me. I was able to sit there and continue to have a good afternoon because I could say to myself, 'I know that comment has nothing to do about me.'

The secret is knowing this universal truth: 'What arises in me is about me'. It means that everything we say and think and do is about us and belongs to us. Everything I say and think and do is about me and belongs to me. As a result, I knew that woman's comments spoke volumes about her feelings about herself rather than about me. Everything we say, every thought we have, reveals our own interior worlds and our own concerns rather than anyone else's. She was feeling bad about herself and projected it onto me.

Clinical psychologist Tony Humphreys describes 'What arises in me is about me' as one of society's best-kept secrets in his insightful book, Relationship, Relationship, Relationship. He warns that if we attempt to point this truth out, the response is often hostile. Sure enough, if I tried to tell that woman that her negative comment about my figure was really about her negative feelings about her own body, the reaction would not have been pleasant.

But whether we like it or not, we reveal ourselves with every thought, word, feeling and action. If we decide to own our thoughts and feelings and comments, then we accept responsibility for our behaviour and actions. We also realise that everyone else's comments are about themselves and learn not to take it personally.

It is a great freedom to know this because it means that no one else can demean, lessen, threaten or reject me. It's only my reaction to others' comments or actions that can reduce me. I realise that if something negative arises in others, it is their problem, their issue. I must take responsibility for anything negative that arises in me and acknowledge that it is my problem. Any negative emotions that arise in me are my feelings about myself and not the other person's.

I remember one occasion in the months after Tom's death when I was out with a few people. A woman, a stranger, came up to me and said to me accusingly: 'I saw you the day after your husband died shopping in Cash's, and you were laughing!'

I had been in Cash's buying a black dress for the funeral. My friend Marian was with me, and maybe Marian said something, and perhaps I did laugh. But that stranger had no idea what was going on in my head and my life. My husband's death crushed me, and I let her comment make me even more distressed.

I recoiled from that woman in shock, and I replayed her comments over and over in my head for a long time afterwards. I don't know what was going on in that woman's life that made her behave so viciously to me, but now I know it was her issue, not mine. I wish I had known that truth then. It would have helped me avoid so much heartache down through the years.

There have been times when I fretted about people and wondered, *why don't they like me?* or *why did they say that?* We can never know what goes on in the minds of other people, but once we accept that everything they say and do is about them, it is a great freedom.

I must remind myself to own my own mistakes and aggressions and fears and stop blaming others too. In the past, there were times when I would get cross with other people, blame them for incompetence when it was my own decisions that I doubted or was concerned about. There have been times when I have reacted angrily to people, and now I realise I was mad at myself, or that I reacted out of fear and insecurity.

If everyone accepted responsibility for their own actions and accepted that everything they do and say speaks volumes about themselves, the world would be such a better place.

It reaches every level in society. Tony Humphreys illustrates in his book what it reveals when a man (or woman) is violent to their partner, for example. We know, of course, that many violent men attribute the blame for their actions to their partners.

'She made me do it' or 'she provoked me' is what they say. Tony interprets domestic violence as a defensive strategy, a fearful, self-protective and unconscious response to childhood trauma and experiences of abandonment. He believes the violent man is trying to control the partner and ensure he or she does not leave or reject him. In the face of continued abandonment as a child, he now forces people to be there for him.

However, the violent man has no awareness of this emotional conflict or threat from his past. His behaviour is unconscious, and he will never accept his actions as his own until he becomes more self-aware. The hope is that if these men receive therapy in a safe, non-judgemental and respectful relationship with a counsellor, they become conscious of why they act like they do and can, therefore, control it.

It's sometimes challenging to remember that I own my own thoughts and behaviour. I need to monitor myself all the time. Sometimes, I'm in company, and I realise that I'm getting irritated by someone who is talking too loudly, for example. I must remind myself, he or she is entitled to speak aloud. The only reason I'm getting irritated is that I don't like that trait in myself. I rarely notice anyone's hair because I love my own hair. But sometimes I catch myself looking critically at another woman's bum, and I realise that's because I'm insecure about mine. I still struggle to stop myself from being judgemental. When I find myself being negative about a person, I try to ask, 'what is that saying about myself?'.

I've had situations where I was not in a good place with myself, and I'd bark at people. I could be downright rude because of what was going on inside me, around my fears and my anxieties. Now I know there's nothing wrong with being fearful, and there's nothing wrong with being anxious, but I need to identify what I'm feeling and not strike out at others because I'm in a bad place. I try to sit with the feelings of fear and anxiety and work out what is it that is making me feel those negative emotions.

Of course, there are times when another's behaviour is hard to accept. If I feel kneejerk disgust or anger towards a person, I try to remind myself that we don't know what is going on in other people's lives. They may be reacting to something traumatic in their lives. They may have been damaged in ways that make them do and say what they do. When people feel shame and can't forgive themselves, the world becomes a hostile, fearful place. They lash out and try to hurt others to relieve their own pain. But once we accept that their behaviour, their actions and what they say is all about *them*, we can step back, remove ourselves and have compassion for them regardless of how their actions or comments affect us.

I don't personalise what other people do and say anymore. I try to catch myself when I am judgemental or when I'm behaving or thinking inappropriately. The world is a much nicer and easier place to be in now. I feel less conflict and turmoil. Cormac and I often talk about this 'secret', and we say if we'd understood the concept of 'what arises in me is about me' years ago, how much easier life would have been!

NEGATIVE PEOPLE, BOUNDARIES AND LABELS

There are times when I've left the company of people, and I've felt bad about myself. I've experienced feelings of hurt, humiliation, frustration or anger, a whole host of negative feelings that lasted for days. My self-esteem and happiness felt lessened.

The term 'toxic' is often used as an unkind label for people who are suffering from a lack of self-worth. These are people who project their pain outwards. They treat others badly because they feel so bad about themselves.

Many people go through life with a complete lack of insight into why they behave as they do. When violent feelings bubble up inside, they never wonder where those feelings come from. When they experience feelings of conflict, anger or pain within them, they feel under attack.

By not accepting responsibility for their own feelings, they place the blame on people around them. People who always feel on the defensive can't see another person's perspective or feel empathy. They start denying all responsibility in situations of conflict. *It's them not me...*

We can all be people like that if we don't accept or understand the concept that everything which *arises in us is about us*. Instead, we believe that everything that arises in us is someone else's fault. We strike out at the people around us. We are constantly angry and blame others for our feelings. Ultimately, we can become negative, sucking all the positivity out of everyone's lives.

I won't accept people like that in my life anymore. If my presence feels lessened by being with another person, I don't want to be there. The truth is, when we finally learn to love and respect ourselves, we will not keep returning to hurtful relationships.

Of course, people continue to remain in unhealthy relationships, and there are many reasons why they do. One of the main ones is out of a sense of duty to their mother, father, brother, sister, husband, wife or child.

If I could shout something from the rooftops, it would be 'mother', 'father', 'brother', 'sister', 'husband' 'wife' and 'child' are nothing but labels!

I cannot bear these labels when they are used as special passes for bad behaviour. Religion tells us to 'honour thy mother and father', and that's wonderful when they honour and respect us too. When there's dignity in the relationship, then it is great. If your parents or siblings or children or spouse is *not* kind or caring, or if they're in a destructive place, why stay there? Why pick up the phone when you know that you're going to experience negativity on the other end?

What purpose does it serve? It just causes pain in your life, and life is too short. We need to remind ourselves that family members are only other human beings like everyone else in our lives.

I had a situation when my poor mum developed dementia, and she became extremely negative and aggressive. It was painful to visit her without feeling absolutely drained. She constantly criticised me, my life or my son, and there was a lot of vitriol. My old self would have fallen to pieces afterwards. I would have taken on board everything my mother said, and I would have taken it personally. When I'm stressed, my immune system suffers, and I get chest infections. The stress of those visits would have brought on one chest infection after another.

The old me would also have reacted defensively and seen my mother's behaviour as an offence or a threat. I would have been rigid and defensive in her company. I might have tried to control or influence her behaviour, arguing with her, telling her this wasn't true.

Or I could have avoided seeing her altogether so that I didn't feel afraid and insecure in the face of this critical onslaught.

But the new me realised that I wanted to keep seeing my mother. It is something that I wouldn't have done for anyone else except my mother. However, to enable me to do that, I had to change my response to her attacks.

First, I had to face my own fears, insecurities and feelings of unworthiness and try to figure out why they were occurring. I knew there was no point in arguing with my mother or in trying to control her behaviour to make myself feel better. I had to understand why I felt so threatened when her behaviour was beyond both her control and mine.

I had to accept that I created these negative feelings myself, and I could create other positive beliefs to replace the negative ones. I also had to accept the feelings that my mother expressed were about her or her dementia. I knew that I was a good daughter and a good person and that I didn't need to feel threatened, upset or disappointed by my mother's words or actions.

The other response I had was to set up a mental boundary. I continued to see my mother and to treat her with respect and dignity. I also responded to her positively when she was open to it. But when she started attacking me or criticising me, I visualised a boundary. A boundary is never rigid like a defence, so my boundary was transparent and perforated, and I would pull it up, so her negative words were muffled. I'd see her mouth move, and I was able to sit with her in compassion and say to myself, 'You poor woman, you are suffering so much. This is all your pain and hurt that you are projecting.' I was able to see her words for what they were: *her* pain and *her* suffering. I didn't personalise it, and I was able to be there for her without harming myself.

We all have a duty to protect ourselves from emotional harm. A boundary, real or imaginary like mine, is a conscious and healthy way to protect ourselves. It's a universal truth that the only person we can change is ourselves. We can't fix others, and family members are no exception. So, *I* make the change by stepping away and lessening my contact with people, family, friends or acquaintances, whose words diminish me. I don't want to be around people who try to get their needs met at the expense of mine.

And once we accept that the only person we can change is ourselves, life becomes a lot easier for us and everyone around us. It is another freedom to understand that the only adult we are responsible for is ourselves. We cannot be responsible for the behaviour of any other adult other than ourselves. People who take me on an emotional rollercoaster ride of negative feelings like pain, guilt, anger, betrayal, obligation or fear do not have to be tolerated or endured, even if they are family.

Letting them go, stepping back, removing ourselves from the situation can be hard sometimes. We can come under attack because of making these changes. I respond by stating my boundaries clearly and calmly: *I need some time for myself; I want some space for myself; I cannot do that now; I will not do that anymore; I am not comfortable with this; I have a hard time listening if you raise your voice; I am not willing to discuss this any further...* The emphasis is on the word 'I' because boundaries call for me to act for myself.

'I' statements are the key to reducing defensiveness because I make my feelings known without hurling accusations or blaming another.

Critical and difficult people are one of life's greatest challenges. I know. My message is to honour ourselves. We owe it to ourselves to stay away from negative energy and anyone or anything that drains us of happiness.

LOOKING AFTER NUMBER ONE

$\mathcal{A}$s a woman, I know I'm inclined to put other people's needs and expectations above my own. Other women tell me they find it hard to say 'no' and find it difficult to prioritise their own needs. When sometimes I have suggested to a client that they look after themselves first, I have heard replies like, 'I'd feel selfish,' or 'How can I put myself first when my poor child is a drug addict?' or 'when my husband is an alcoholic' or 'when my mother is so sick?'

Self-care is not selfish. It's not about being pampered in a beauty salon by masseurs and therapists. It is recognising that you have a duty to love yourself and care

for yourself first. Even the Bible recognises the importance of loving yourself when it advocates 'Love thy neighbour as *thyself.' Thyself.* The gospel starts from a premise that you must love yourself. Self-care may sound indulgent, but it is critical for everyone's overall well-being.

It's like the oxygen mask safety rule that we hear every time we fly: 'In the event of a sudden loss in cabin pressure, oxygen masks will drop down from the overhead compartment. Please place the mask over your own mouth and nose before assisting others.' They tell this to protect capable adults from passing out or dying while trying to help others who are confused and struggling.

The message is clear: It is only when I take care of myself that I can help others. And once I can love 'me' unconditionally, it enables me to love others unconditionally. We try not to let ourselves take second place because the only adult we are responsible for is ourselves.

Yet, we can be people-pleasers and overcommit instead of saying 'no'. There are people who have a lack of self-awareness or self-worth. And guilt is often the biggest obstacle to self-care. *How can I do X for myself when Y needs me?*

How many times have we seen frazzled mothers yelling at their kids, clearly stressed and anxious? If our brains are in over-drive, and we can't sleep, or we're snapping at people, that's a red flag. Shouting at people or resenting them is not helping them. Those mothers shouting at their children would be better off asking a friend or family member to babysit and going to bed for the afternoon.

Sometimes, we need to take time out and turn off our phones, ignore our inboxes and shirk all the demands on us. To do this might entail asking for help with our kids or elderly parents or our work colleagues. We may also need to establish boundaries when it comes to the demands of other people or our jobs.

If we're feeling stressed, we must learn to re-prioritise ourselves. Find 'me-time' - go for a walk, turn off the phone for a weekend, go to the beauty salon, have that lie-in, read that book. If we are burnt-out, exhausted, full or regret or resentfulness, we are not only harming ourselves but the people around us.

I cannot say this often enough: The only adult we are responsible for is ourselves. Self-care matters. We feel well when we reduce stress, eat well, exercise and sleep well, and we have to relax to stay healthy, happy and resilient. It's only when we feel well that we can be effective enough to help those around us who really need us.

THE PROBLEM WITH ADVICE

J recently read an interview with the husband of Michaela Harte who was brutally murdered on their honeymoon in Mauritius in 2011. John McAreavey, who still seeks justice for Michaela, says he receives messages on social media all the time advising him that it's time to 'get over this'.

John has remarried, but that doesn't mean he doesn't want to honour the memory of his late wife. He has a burning desire to find the truth behind the murder of his late wife. That's who he is.

Anyone who loves him and cherishes him is going to say, 'that's okay. This is who you are, and I am going to support you.'

Because 'it's time to move on' is probably the cruellest thing you can say to somebody when they're struggling with grief in their lives. No one simply 'gets over it'. The experience of great loss changes us deeply and forever.

Yet, perfectly well-meaning people will advise people reeling with pain that 'it's time to move on' or 'it's in the past' or 'get on with your life.' It was said to me in times when I was in a very dark place. I heard remarks like: 'You have to move on now for the sake of your child.'

And I remember that it made me feel like there was something wrong with me because I couldn't snap back to my old self. It meant that on top of being heartbroken, I also felt guilty and inadequate. This 'advice' made me feel like I was failing; the message I internalised was that I was a weak person because I couldn't move on.

What I needed back then was care, compassion and kindness. That's all anyone seeks when they are suffering. The last thing I wanted was this unasked for 'advice' that made me feel worse than I already felt. No one who is grieving deserves to be told to 'move on'.

To me, doling out unsolicited advice is downright rude in any situation. It means that we are trying to manage what isn't ours to manage. Those at the receiving end of unasked for advice often end up feeling more stressed, offended or irritated because what we say comes across as criticism. We hurt their feelings because we are basically. saying we are smarter than them. We know the answers. We are telling them that we know what is best for them, which we never do.

I remember coming out of Mass in my local church one day, and a woman I vaguely knew approached me. I had been in hospital after a particularly bad bout of COPD. I must work at keeping myself straight and standing erect anyway, but after being so sick with a chest infection, I looked a bit stooped. I was still weak, and I wasn't feeling great.

Anyway, this woman marched right up to me outside the church. 'Marion,' she said. 'I was watching you in Mass, and you are wearing this beautiful outfit, but your shoulders are so hunched. You would really want to straighten up.'

I was stunned. Why on earth did this woman feel that she was entitled to give me unasked for advice? She had no idea of my circumstances or that I was just out of hospital after being terribly ill. We never know what's going on in other people's lives or their minds. I was struggling. What I needed was care and compassion, not criticism and being told to 'straighten up'!

These days, I try never to advise unless I'm asked. It's a type of arrogance to assume we know what is best for another. We never do. The only person who knows what's right for them is that person themselves. Even if I see people who are struggling, I know the last thing they need is advice. They know what is wrong with their lives, and they are doing the best they can.

The only time I give advice now is when I'm paid to do it as an image consultant. I don't even see it as advice. My job, as I see it, is to highlight all the positives in a person. We are all perfect the way we are, and I repeat that to my clients all the time. My job is to enhance people's God-given natural beauty and inspire them to look and feel their best.

Of course, I meet so many women who complain their legs are too short, or their bum is too big. My message is clear: I never met anybody whose body isn't perfect as it is. People are very hard on themselves, and it's challenging to battle that critical inner voice that we all hear. I have clients who arrive feeling bad because they've put on weight or lost too much weight or their hair is thinning, or their skin is breaking out. But I see it as my job to make them feel fantastic as they walk out.

I'd certainly never tell someone to 'straighten up'. The only type of 'advice' that is acceptable is asked for advice or advice that is positive and encouraging.

Of course, years ago, I would have been first in the queue to dole out advice, and the habits of a lifetime are hard to break. I'm the eldest in a family, so I think I know everything. I have to bite my tongue so many times, as I'm about to say 'Well if I were in your shoes, I would do this...' I'm a mother, and it's hard not to advise especially when it comes to my own son.

But I believe that living your best life and being a decent human being means never advising unless someone asks.

Now, if I have to say anything to a person who is struggling, I make sure it is something that makes them feel better about themselves. I always aim to support a person in pain rather than advise them.

Better still, I know from my own darkest days, that the best way to help a person and support them is by listening. As that hit song goes, You Say it Best When You Say Nothing at All.

WHEN YOU SAY NOTHING AT ALL

*T*he nights are hard when you lose someone close to you. When Tom died, I dreaded the night-time. During the day, I tried to appear normal. I'd fill the hours looking after my child and meeting friends and family. But after 6.00pm, when I closed the front door and put Tom Junior to bed, I found the silence and the stillness oppressive.

For me, it was always after dark that I really felt the void that Tom left. The loneliness caused by grief hit me hard at night, especially during the winter. It felt like everyone around me was getting back to 'normal', but I wasn't. The clock ticked heavily and slowly after dark, and the nights seemed endless.

I had one friend who was a beacon of light for me during those terrible nights. Her name is Mary Groeger, and she is my dear friend. I remember she was breastfeeding her child in the months after Tom's death. She would drive over to me after her last feed of the night before she went to bed. I remember her arriving even on the coldest, wildest nights in the rain, and her visits were my salvation. My spirits would lift as soon as I heard her knock on the door. Knowing that she was going to come and break the monotony of an evening alone meant so much.

And what, in hindsight, meant even more to me, is that she never, ever gave advice. She never said much at all. She just sat with me and listened. It was such a gift during those dark days in my life. When everyone else was trying to tell me what to do, how to live and telling me how I needed to 'move on' with my life, she just listened. By doing that, she affirmed my feelings, let me know that she understood and that my emotions were legitimate. During times when I thought I might be going mad, to have someone to listen was such a gift.

I believe listening is the greatest gift you can give another. It's invaluable to someone who is suffering to be able to talk, without being judged, criticised or advised.

It's hard to be a listener, though. I've had friends who have had partners I disapproved of, for example. I'd think, *what on earth does she see in him?* The day would usually arrive when that friend arrived at my door, upset and complaining that their partner said *this*, and did *that*. The first thing I would have done in the past is say, 'Why are you with him? You know he's no good for you. You deserve better.'

All this friend really wanted was to know that I was there for her and that I supported her. She didn't want my 'advice' that effectively criticised her choices and questioned her faculties.

We're all smart people who know what's best for ourselves. We know consciously or unconsciously when something isn't right, and we'll make the right decisions for ourselves when the time is right.

As we're working our way through solving our issues, we just want somebody to hear us and have a bit of compassion and to hold us. We don't need judgement. We wish to be heard. That's all any of us desire when it comes to friendship.

These days, I shut up when I see people in a situation that I rather they weren't in. I have learnt to accept this is their journey, their life and they must live it. It's tough, though, and I have to resort to prayer sometimes to help me to be non-judgmental.

I remember when someone close to me was going through an appalling time a few years ago. Like most people, when I see someone in a lot of pain, I don't like standing by feeling helpless. This person never asked for help, but my instinct was to rush in and take over and try to sort everything out myself.

I was studying relationship mentoring, and I knew this wasn't the appropriate response. I even talked to a lecturer about it. He reiterated, 'Don't try and fix them, don't give advice, don't criticise. Hear them, show compassion and kindness and let them know you are there for them. But they are the only ones who can fix it.' He also urged, 'Try to hold them where they're at.'

So, I restrained myself. I reminded myself that I have no responsibility for and no control over any other adult's decisions. I realise now that when we try to step outside of our own business, we have no power to affect change. It's a waste of time and energy. Instead, I focus on the things that are mine to manage, and I try to help others now by just listening.

Of course, listening is a skill, and like acquiring any skill, it requires practice. I still find it hard to sit and listen and not to interrupt with: 'If I were in your shoes, I would do this...'

I keep reminding myself I have no idea what I would do if I were in their shoes. I am never going to be in their shoes. I only know what to do for myself.

So, to be the best person that I can be, I let people talk, and I make them feel safe. They know their problems are not going to leave the room, and I'm always there for them.

If they are depressed and can't talk, I just sit with them. It makes people feel less alone in the dark if someone sits beside them, waiting for the sun to come up. Just being there for someone and listening is real love.

OUR SUPERPOWER!

*H*ow often are we told, 'follow your head, not your heart' when it comes to making important decisions? Clear, rational and conscious reasoning is often valued over our intuitive feelings.

Yet how many times have we hear the phrases: 'I should have listened to my gut feeling' and 'I had a hunch, and it was right.'

To me, gut instinct or that inner voice is a kind of human super-power. There are times in life where everything on the surface appears fine, and yet I've thought 'this still doesn't feel quite right.' I've learnt not to question that instinct.

If my inner voice is urging caution, I consider it valid information. Gut feelings help me to decide whether to trust someone or whether to back away from a situation that doesn't feel quite right. For millennia, human beings' survival depended on their instincts to ward off potentially harmful situations.

In times of crisis, I will always listen to my intuition because it usually kicks in when we need it most. Our' sixth sense' is often a very valuable tool in our arsenal of self-defence, so I never discount it.

Of course, it's easy to get overwhelmed in a time of crisis. Responsibilities weigh upon us and we are bombarded with conflicting feelings and the sounds of others' voices. Our intuition can get drowned out by the noise.

Whenever I'm conflicted, I try to sit quietly with the issue, meditation upon it, walk in nature and do whatever I can to release stress.

Then I listen to what my gut is telling me, and it is usually right. Our sixth sense is a superpower at our disposal once we learn to listen to it.

CONQUERING DARK TIMES

I remember one of the first times I went to see a psychotherapist, and I told him that I was suffering from depression. He replied, 'Depression is only a label'. I remember feeling stunned and hurt by what he said because it sounded so glib. Depression felt like a lot more than a label to me then. It's only in more recent years that I understand what he meant.

'Depression' is an all-encompassing umbrella term that describes symptoms that affect us emotionally, physically, spiritually and mentally. Sadness, grief, depression, or just feeling down in the dumps - whatever we choose to call it - is part of being human.

We all face regrets, losses, disappointments so feeling down is as inevitable as the tide ebbing and flowing. However, our levels of hurt and pain are different at different times in our lives. After Tom's death and after my miscarriages, I experienced a range of symptoms of such intensity that it took over my life. There were times when I felt almost disabled by fear and anxiety, and I felt suicidal. I would have been happy to go to bed and know that I would never wake up.

Holocaust survivor, Viktor Frankl wrote a memoir, Man's Search for Meaning on his horrific experiences in Auschwitz. He explored why it was that some people in the concentration camps gave up and died while others survived the same conditions. He explained it using the Friedrich Nietzsche quote: 'He who has a 'why' to live can bear almost any how.' It meant those people who were able to find meaning in their lives, who identified a purpose in life had a more positive outcome. Some people strove to keep their children alive or refused to give up thoughts of seeing their families again survived the camps. You can put up with almost anything in life if you have a 'why'.

After Tom died, I could willingly have let my life end, but I had a 'why' with my son. I despaired and wondered if the darkness would ever lift, but I survived it because I had my child to live for.

We all need a 'why' to survive the worst of depression. Some people struck by tragedy have poured their energies into fundraising or establishing a charity in the name of their loved ones. Others have found a purpose in life by joining the Samaritans or training for a marathon or rescuing pets from their local animal pound. Everyone has their way to cope, but it's crucial to find and focus on a 'why' or meaning in our lives during periods of terrible pain and trauma.

It's also important to acknowledge that what we are experiencing, that despair, that sick feeling in the pit of the stomach, that sense of black oppression and hopelessness, is normal. It is part of the process of grief.

Unfortunately, when I was grieving, I felt my reaction was a weakness. I was ashamed by how I felt, so I made myself socialise at times when I was miserable. I forced a smile on my face when my heart was breaking. I needed professional help and counselling, but I was too ashamed to seek it out. Thank God for people like Niall 'Bressie' Breslin who are telling the world that this all-encompassing label of 'depression' applies to most people at some stage in their lives.

I know now that depression is not a weakness but can be an inner friend trying to tell me something. It's a signal, a flashing warning light, that something needs to be looked at and addressed in my life. It's telling me negative emotions of some sort are taking over and that I need to identify and handle the situation.

I don't suffer from crushing depression anymore, but I do have days when I feel in a low mood, and the world just seems to cloud over. But with my new perspective on depression, I know it's not something to be fearful of. Depression is a form of intuition; it is an inner voice telling me there's something not right in my life that I need to fix.

It urges me to get to the root of the negative emotion I am experiencing - fear, anger, sadness, loneliness. - Once I discover the root cause, I can tackle the problem.

The best way to find the root of this 'dis-ease' is mindful listening and self-care. For me, depression is a message, waiting for a response. I always ask, *why am I feeling like this?* I usually find the answer when I wait. Once I identify the emotion inside me, I feel I am half-way to feeling better already. It's important to recognise my feelings, honour them and express them.

Sometimes our emotions are so great or are buried so deep within us that we need professional help. In these cases, a compassionate and skilled therapist can help us uncover those issues so we can process them, express our feelings and move on in life.

And sometimes we must accept that the trauma we feel is not even our own. Research is showing that the destructive effects of trauma are passed down from generation to generation. Scientists in the emerging field called epigenetics have proved trauma and tragedy can be passed down for at least three generations.

It's known, for example, that anxious mothers can raise the cortisol levels in the amniotic fluid, transferring these high-stress hormones to their babies in the womb. Eminent psychiatrist, Dr Gabor Maté, who was born to a Jewish mother during Nazi-occupied Hungary, related a story that his mother told him. When he was six-months old, she brought him to a doctor and pleaded with the doctor to help her.

'I can't stop my baby crying,' she said. 'He never stops crying. I've followed all the advice, but he's crying non-stop.'

The doctor simply shook his head and said: 'All the Jewish babies are crying.'

It seems certain now that generations of people can unconsciously inherit and carry traumas and destructive patterns of behaviour down their ancestral line.

For me, the root problem of my depression in the past was loneliness. I realise now that I wasn't suffering from the label 'depression' so much as I was suffering from loneliness. I don't mean that I was suffering from being alone. I like being alone a lot of the time, but loneliness is a very different thing. I have been in a room full of people at parties, and the loneliness has nearly choked me. I felt physical pain from missing the love, the holding and the tenderness of somebody so integral and vital to my life.

After Tom died, the loneliness, the hurt and the fear was crippling in its intensity. When my boy left to go to college and then left the country to move to Hong Kong, I felt very lonely too. For many, many years, Tom's anniversary was very painful for me. It brought all this loneliness back.

I believe loneliness is the cause of a lot of depression or 'dis-ease' in the world. And I understand now that there's always a reason when I feel low. Once I remove the label of depression and identify what I'm feeling, I can say it's okay to feel like this. I also know that I can handle it and that it's going to pass.

I have a friend who anticipates the arrival of these dark days. She'll say: 'That bloody black dog is outside the door. I'm not letting him in, but he's fighting to get in the door.'

She might call me the next day and say: 'He got in, that son of a bitch.'

I'll say: 'Sit with it, hon. You'll find out what's going on, and you'll be able to kick him out in a few days.' And she always does. She finds the source of these negative feelings that have arisen in her, and then she tackles it.

I go to Lanzarote in the winter for my health and to escape the worst effects of COPD, but Cormac has businesses to run in Ireland. As much as I enjoy my own company, I love my husband's company as well, and I'd much rather the two of us were together. So, I am mindful of my mood. I am careful not to slip into a feeling of melancholy when he's gone.

Even if I do start feeling low, I know it's just a passing phase. Once I identify the root of what's troubling me, I can address the problem, and the depression goes.

In the meanwhile, I find the trick is to be gentle with myself. I try to do whatever makes me feel good when I feel bad. If I'm having a bad day, I might pull the blanket over my head or eat that packet of biscuits. Bad days are only made worse by being hard on ourselves. I indulge myself, and I make no excuses for it.

I remember years ago going down Castle Street in Cork pushing the baby in the buggy in the lashing rain. Somehow, the buggy and I slipped from the footpath and landed with a splash in the gutter. It was just a minor incident, but it was after Tom's death, and I remember crying on the street. I said: 'Oh sweetheart of Jesus, is this pain ever going to lift?' Then I thought about a ring that

I'd seen in the jewellers' window on Oliver Plunkett Street. I had talked myself out of buying it earlier by thinking, *I don't need it.* I pulled ourselves back onto the pavement, and I thought, *I'm buying the bloody ring.* I turned the buggy around, and I went back and bought the ring. And it cheered me. I did something for myself that made me feel better, and that's okay.

In later years, I have taken anti-depressants, and they did help. I'd have no problem taking them again if I was going through another crisis.

Creativity is also a great distraction when I'm feeling low. Painting and creating can slow my mind and help me hear the message that my inner self is trying to share with me. Some people can lose themselves in adult colouring books or hobbies. Making money is my hobby, so I craft stones and wood into ornaments and sell them in the local gallery and craft store. I also make earrings by hand, and I can lose myself for hours doing that. I get totally absorbed when I'm doing my arts and crafts, and it is an excellent way to calm my mind and relax.

There's a proverb that says, 'When there is no enemy within, the enemies outside can do you no harm.' Negative emotions like anxiety, stress, fear, jealousy and anger can be the enemy within. 'Depression' is the ally that tells us that the enemy is taking over. I know that once I mindfully listen and identify the negative feelings, I'm no longer controlled by them. It's another great freedom in life to know that with a little gentle self-reflection and self-care, I have the power to conquer most of the negativity and darkness in my life.

CRUTCHES, DRUGS AND ESCAPE HATCHES

*T*en years ago, I woke up after a night before with a ball of anxiety lodged in the pit of my stomach. I thought: *That's it! I'm never drinking again.* But this time I meant it.

I can't go into detail about the event that precipitated this pledge because it involved other people. Let's just say I ended up in a verbal altercation that wouldn't have happened if I wasn't drinking.

I often questioned my relationship with alcohol before that morning. All down through the years, I never drank at home, but it was always a vital social crutch when I went out at weekends. People find it hard to believe that I was shy socially because I could get up in front of people, speak in public and present a course. The thing is that I had great self-belief and confidence business-wise, but socially, my self-assurance and spirit was shattered after Tom died.

In the months and years after I lost my husband, going out drinking was not only my only social outlet but was also a way to avoid emotions like sadness, loneliness and anger. I have a lot of compassion and sympathy for my younger self as a thirty-year-old widow, a woman crucified by emotional pain.

Alcohol was a coping tool and a great way to numb all those negative feelings. Any dependency or addiction, whether it's gambling, drugs, sex or alcohol, is a release. It's a diversion from something negative that is happening in our lives. Drink was a social lubricant, which lifted me out of myself and made me feel like the life and soul of the party at times.

Monday to Friday, I was a mother and a businesswoman, and there was never any alcohol in the house. I also always gave up drink for Lent every year, and I always give it up for the month of the Holy Souls for Tom every November. But towards the end it of those droughts, it was still a case of, 'Will this ever be over so I can have a drink?' There was no problem going back on it.

Whenever I thought about giving up drink, I quickly forgot about it. I feared that I'd be bored, or worse still, that I'd be boring. This went on for years.

When I began studying and went to college, I embarked on a new journey of self-discovery and personal growth. It gradually began to dawn on me that I needed to stop worrying about other people and start looking after myself.

When I learnt to be at one with myself, I was in a more peaceful place, and it became easier to address my relationship with alcohol.

Drinking is so acceptable in our society. Many of us shake our heads at the use of drugs like cocaine and heroin, failing to recognise that alcohol is a far more destructive drug in this country.

I had to accept that drink wasn't doing me any favours in the end. It wasn't something that brought me peace. Yes, it was fun at times, but it was also destructive, and if I was in a bad place, I could be contrary. I didn't like myself sometimes when I was drinking, and the last time I drank, I certainly didn't like myself. And those few hours of socialising left me feeling depressed, lethargic and generally unwell afterwards.

So, after waking up that fateful morning, I decided the first thing to do was to commit to my decision to never drink alcohol again. I thought the best way to do that was to start telling everyone I was giving up drink.

I remember ringing my son and saying, 'Tom, I've given up the drink. I've made up my mind, and I'm giving it up.'

He didn't miss a beat.

'So, what did you do, Mum?' he said.

I didn't think he was very fair at the time, but in a way, he was right. It was like you have to hit rock bottom before you get your act together.

Shortly afterwards, I met a very good friend of mine who lived on Reenaroga Island, where we had our weekend holiday home at the time.

'Kathleen, I'm giving up the drink,' I announced, delighted with myself.

I'll never forget her reply because it stunned me.

'I'm glad, Marion,' she said. 'You're to the nicest person in the world until you have four drinks, then I don't like you anymore.'

If ever I needed something to strengthen my resolve, her response was it.

I prayed a lot because I knew it would be difficult to give up the habit of a lifetime, and I went for counselling. I felt I needed a period of self-reflection if I was breaking up with alcohol for good. I wasn't exactly struggling with giving up alcohol, but it was a significant change. Our social life every weekend revolved around places that were known for good food and wine.

The first few weekends of being sober, I decided to stay at home and get used to it. However, I didn't want to interfere with Cormac's weekends.

'This is not your journey, Cormac,' I said. 'This is about me. Please, go out and meet everyone as usual.'

So, Cormac did go out, and he came back late, like we normally did. The following Saturday night, Cormac went out, but he came back a bit earlier. The third weekend night he went out, he was only gone an hour when I heard him come back in the door.

'You know what, I've decided I can't be bothered,' he said. 'Once we're together, I'm happy. I don't need to go out, and I don't want to go without you.' Cormac was never a big drinker anyway, but that was a great support. Maybe if he had been continuously going out to the pub, I wouldn't have been as strong.

Prayer was always important to me, and I was attracted to the faith-based approach of Alcoholics Anonymous, so I decided to go there too.

I remember walking into the first AA meeting, wearing cerise pink from head to toe. It was raining outside, and I even had a cerise umbrella. I looked around and never felt more conspicuous in my life. Everyone in the room seemed to be wearing grey, and I looked like a flashing pink beacon. I went there thinking that I wouldn't know anybody in the place. So, I walked up to the reception table and said, 'Excuse me, I haven't been here before - what do I do?' And the man who turned around was related to me!

I appreciated the support and the prayerful atmosphere. I heard many cautionary accounts from people who lost families, homes and businesses. I never spoke while I was there, but some of the stories I heard were harrowing. It brought home to me the harm that can come with alcohol abuse. Yet, I was still worried about my resolve.

I still couldn't imagine every weekend for the rest of my life without ever having a drink again.

Praying is one of my passions, and I find having spirituality in my life incredibly calming and positive. I have great faith in Our Lady, and I have great faith in prayer. I meditate, and I go to yoga, but the greatest peace I get is when I recite the Holy Rosary during my walk. That's who I am, and that's what I love. When I'm saying the Rosary as I'm walking, my mind is full of nature and spirit and kindness and goodness. The Rosary is important to me.

One night, I turned out the light after saying the Rosary, expecting a good night's sleep. But hours later, I woke again; something had disturbed me. I opened my eyes, blinking in confusion, and saw an orange light in the bedroom, a warm glowing aura at the end of the bed.

I shook Cormac in fright,

'Cor? Cor? Look! Can you see that?'

He roused himself.

'What love?'

'Can you see the light?'

'What light?'

All I can say is that I was filled with this overwhelming, unbeliev-able feeling of love. I can't describe it, because it was so incredible, so beautiful. It was all-encompassing love.

I don't know who it was or what it was. All I know is that I would have happily gone with the light, the feeling was so magnificent. Some might describe it as a religious or mystical experience. The Catholic Church refers to 'locutions', forms of private revelations or a supernatural communication. I don't know what to call 'it'. It just happened. The feeling of love and peace that visited me that night was like nothing I'd ever experienced in my life before. And then the light went and brought the feeling of unbelievable love with it.

'Did you feel that, hon?' I asked Cormac. 'Did you feel that energy, that love?' It seemed to pulse through the room. I couldn't believe it, but he saw and felt nothing.

'Cormac, I'm never going to drink again,' I said, and I knew it for a fact. I knew from that instant that the struggle was over. Whatever or whoever came to me, whether it was Tom or my dad or the Holy Spirit or Our Lady, I was free. I got to a place where I was one with myself, and I realised that I didn't want alcohol in my life anymore. And I'll tell you, not drinking is the most fabulous feeling in the world.

Cormac and I still go to all the parties, all the events, and we stay out all night and have a ball. I'll usually be the first out of the dance floor. It wouldn't enter my head now that I need alcohol to enjoy myself anymore. At the same time, I've no problem with anybody else drinking, absolutely no problem. It's only when it becomes destructive, and it's negative that it becomes a problem. I was out with pals who had four bottles of wine between two of them the other day, and they were great fun. There was nothing said that was cruel or unkind, but I am glad to have put alcohol behind me.

I see a lot of other people struggling with drink in this country. People drink habitually even though their minds are unconsciously telling them to quit. Mine tried to tell me to quit for a long time, and for a long time I ignored it! It's a drug, and it's hard to give up drugs. My heart goes out to people who still feel like alcohol is a friend or a joy in their lives when it's hurting them. The sad thing is that there are people who drink a bottle of wine every night and fail to realise that they are hooked on a drug.

There are lots of different kinds of drugs out there. For some people, alcohol is their drug, for others it's hash or cocaine. A lot of people struggle with gambling now especially with online gambling. Other people can't make the break from nicotine. 'Oh, I only smoke one or two a day,' I hear all the time from people who can't accept that they're still smokers.

Of course, there are others of us who have a bad relationship or obsession with food. I know myself that I eat mindlessly when I'm sitting around and watching TV whereas when I'm crafting or absorbed in a book, that doesn't happen at all.

For some of us, pornography, sex, Valium or other prescription pills are our drugs. For others, their fix is shopping. They're all drugs, all crutches so that we can cope with the road bumps in life. They are escape hatches to avoid facing stress, pressure or events or feelings in our lives that have become overwhelming. We are self-medicating, using these behaviours or substances to help to numb the pain.

When we're happy indulging in our 'drug', our guilty pleasure every so often, that's fine. When this drug starts causing hurt and pain to us or others, then it's time to reconsider our 'coping' strategies. Often, we see our drug of choice as a coping 'solution' until we are forced to accept it has become the real problem.

I try not to give unwanted advice to people, but if you're wondering whether you have a problem with a substance or a behaviour of any sort, you probably have. If these 'drugs' are causing problems, controlling us or interfering with our peace of mind, I suggest that we address them. We have the resources within ourselves to be in a good place, to be in a healthy place both physically and mentally.

I wish I had stopped drinking a lot sooner, because I've discovered a new sense of freedom. I feel a lot lighter these days. Alcohol is a drug that no longer has any claim on my life. I have my weekends back, especially my Sundays, and I can focus on all the positive things around me. I am in a lovely, peaceful place and feel blessed. Putting drink behind me, makes me feel as if I won the lotto in life, and that I'm the luckiest woman on the planet!

WE ARE WHERE WE ARE MEANT TO BE

How often have you heard the term that someone was in 'the wrong place at the wrong time?' When life deals us a bad hand, we often believe that it was unfair. We believe it was some cruel cosmic joke that should have never happened. Then we read or we hear someone say, 'we are where we are meant to be' and we think, 'Really? Am I meant to be sad and miserable and angry?'

Yet often it's the difficulties and those rough patches in our lives that trigger the metamorphoses that change life for the better. I have experienced these triggers in the past. Chronic illness is often a way of telling us that we need to care more for ourselves. Deep depression can be a sign that our levels of job stress are too high. The death of someone close to us is a warning that our time is running out for us too. Without experiencing pain and tragedy, we may never develop the empathy and compassion that we need to care for others.

Sometimes it takes a whole gamut of personal disasters to make us wake up and realise that we are where we are meant to be. Maybe, we have been drifting and haven't been questioning our direction in life. Sometimes bad news is just a lesson from life, a signpost to remind us we are going in the wrong way. This lesson can become a terrible struggle when we resist it. However, if we trust that we are where we are meant to be, then all these incidents, good and bad, are okay. They are temporary twists and turns on the road. Every obstacle helps us learn a little more, breaks us and builds us so we can push through and try to get to where we want to be, or we imagine we want to be.

Without the struggles and challenges I've had in my life, I wouldn't be the person I am now. I wouldn't have the life I have or reached the levels of happiness and contentment that I have. I get through life more easily now by releasing my vice grip on 'plans' and accepting that life changes, and life can surprise me in good and bad ways. I am where I am meant to be.

Sometimes, when life deals me a great hand, I can worry too. I have been living in West Cork, surrounded by nature and the ocean, and I am with someone I adore. In the summer, I walk the tranquil country roads filled with the electric pink blooms of rhododendron and fuchsia and the saffron flash of montbretia. All year round, there are the soft blues and greens of heather and gorse which is rustled by the fresh, salt breeze of the Atlantic Ocean. It feels like a surfeit of riches. Sometimes I feel a pang of worry or guilt. I think, *Really? Am I meant to be so happy? Do I deserve all this happiness?*

Then I remember, and I know everything is unfolding exactly as it should. I say to myself, *this is good. This is okay. I am right where I am meant to be.*

PART III
THE GLORIOUS COLOUR MAKEOVER

MARION'S COLOUR MAKEOVER

*B*efore we embark on this journey, beginning in colour and continuing through style and image, I wish to emphasise that we are not our bodies. We are far more than the size we are and far more than the shape we are. We are more than a style or a mere palette of colours. We are here, and we matter!

We are fabulous beings with hearts, souls, minds and spirits. Our bodies and faces are something we wear for a while and I believe they are to be cherished while we have them. And it is life-enhancing to be able to display them with love, confidence and pride every day.

Because our God-given bodies and faces are perfect, whatever size and shape they are.

When we learn about colour, image and style, it helps us identify clothes and cosmetics that are complementary to our natural beauty. Having this knowledge helps us understand at a glance what clothes and make-up will have us looking our absolute best.

By the end of this book, my hope is to have imparted a greater understanding and appreciation of the physical part of our divine selves.

If we can all be inspired to look and feel our best, I believe we can live with more joy and fulfilment in our lives.

THE BEAUTY OF A COLOUR MAKEOVER

We have all admired glorious sunsets of reds and oranges, and we've stared in awe at the magnificent blue of the sky as it blends into the ocean.

Did you know that mother nature not only creates the most harmonious colour palettes in landscapes, but in people? Colour analysis teaches us that we are all born with hair, skin tone and eyes that contrast or blend together to create a unique work of art.

We are all beautiful the way we're made. However, we can enhance ourselves, like any work of art, by good framing. Our frames are fashion and make-up and when they are chosen well, they can bring out the natural beauty we are all born with.

I never heard of personal colour analysis until I went to Canada and stayed with a friend, Jean, who had already been to see a colour consultant.

She was a social worker so she wore smart, professional clothes to work every day. Straight away, I noticed how she made dressing stylishly for work look effortless. Her blended wardrobe of warm beiges, light browns and off-white colours seemed so minimalist chic.

I saw her walk out that door every morning, exuding profession-alism and confidence, in what seemed like an endless array of outfits. But when she opened her wardrobe, she showed me that she had only about a dozen pieces which she mixed and matched to great effect every day.

'You have such nice clothes, but your colours are all over the place,' she said. I didn't have a notion what she was talking about, but I knew I wanted to learn her shopping skills. Everything she owned looked great on her and mixed and matched with everything else she had. Meanwhile, my wardrobe was jammed with beautiful clothes, but they didn't work together and many didn't make me look or feel good.

So, I booked an appointment with the woman's colour consultant, and the veils lifted from my eyes. Colour analysis was a revelation and yet, it was so simple. It was all about finding harmony with the natural colours in our hair, skin tones and eyes. It all made sense at last.

When a woman isn't aware of the colour palette that works for her, two things might happen: *She may buy a lot of clothes that she never wears, and she may have a lot of clothes that look dull and uninteresting on her.* I know this because I was that person before I trained. I was that woman who had wardrobes of clothes and still felt like I had nothing to wear.

Down through the years, I've come across people who are reluctant to have their colours 'done'.

'I don't want to be told what colour I can and can't wear!' they say.

Let me make this clear, personal colour analysis is not about dictating who gets to wear what colour. Everybody can wear almost every colour. The colour analysis journey is about helping us find the tone and shade of those colours that best suits our own natural colouring.

Walk into a paint shop and look at the swatches of green colours and we will find hundreds if not thousands of variations of green. Some of those shades may look awful when applied to the walls of our home and some, depending on the light and the material in the wall, will look amazing.

It works the same for people. Those with lighter skin, hair and eyes are enhanced by lighter, softer colours. Meanwhile, those with darker features can make their hair, skin and eyes pop with deeper, richer colours.

If light-featured person wears dark colours, their delicate looks are overwhelmed. Bold and deep colours on light-featured people high-light the shadows under their eyes and round the mouth. Alternatively, it is not flattering for someone with dark eyes and hair to wear light, muted colours.

The simplest way of explaining it is that our wardrobe and makeup look best on us if they work in harmony with our natural features.

Once we work out our natural colours, we have the key to looking and feeling great because we are armed with the palette of colours that complements the looks we're born with.

We all have to wear clothes, so why not choose colours and styles that make us look fabulous?

Once we unlock the secrets of our colours, looking more radiant, vibrant and confident is made easy.

THE MAKEUP CATEGORIES

*H*ave you ever applied foundation and ended up with an orange-hued face? That's probably because you have a warm-toned foundation that is mixing badly with the blue tones in your skin.

Or have you applied foundation that has made you look grey and unwell? That may be because you are trying to use a blue-based cool foundation on warm skin.

Similarly, a light-featured face can be overwhelmed by heavy black eyeliner. And a woman with wonderful dark hair and eyes can look washed out wearing even the most fashionable pale pink lipstick.

The beauty of colour analysis is that it helps us identify the shades of makeup that will enhance *US* rather than the cosmetic companies' profit margins!

8 REASONS TO KNOW OUR COLOURS

- It will save us a fortune in clothes. Believe me, we won't come home again with an item of clothes that we will never wear. There will be no more expensive mistakes, because the more we know, the less we need!
- It will save us a fortune in make-up. Once we have the right colour palette for us, there will be no more bad lipstick choices and no more wasted blushers and eye-shadows.
- Shopping becomes a far easier experience. We can avoid the rails filled with the shades or colours that we know will do nothing to enhance our looks and hone in on those rails that carry our colours. We can steer away from all the lipsticks that overwhelm or underwhelm our looks. The guessing game is over!
- There will be no more dithering over the hair-colour samples at the hair salon. We will know straight away the tones to make us look fab.
- We will have far more to wear even though we buy less. Our wardrobe will become more streamlined, but all our clothes will complement or contrast

- Wearing the right colour palette for our skin complexion, hair and eyes will make us look healthier and more vibrant. We learn which shades detract from our lovely complexions and make us look washed out.
- Colour has energy and so does confidence. When we look our best, we feel better and we exude more life and sparkle. We become more self-assured. We can take on the world once we feel confident!
- Do colour analysis once, and we understand our colours for life unless we decide to swing to a completely different hair colour. The returns in the investment in ourselves are multiplied many times over!

WHAT COLOUR CATEGORY AM I?

*O*nce we discover the colours that are in harmony with our skin, hair and eyes colours, we look brighter, lighter and our smiles are whiter!

So how do we figure out which of the twelve colour categories do we belong to?

The first steps to discovering the best colour palette for our features involve analysing whether our features are warm or cool, light or deep and soft or clear.

Steps to Finding Our Colour Category

Colour analysis begins by assessing the colours of our features – our complexion, hair and eyes - and asking three questions:

- *Are the colours of our features warm or cool?*
- *Are the colours of our features light or deep?*
- *Are the colours of our features soft or clear?*

The most prominent two of these six characteristics will determine which of the twelve categories we belong to.

Colour consultant at work

WARM OR COOL COLOURING

ARE THE COLOURS OF OUR FEATURES WARM OR COOL?

Warm skin tones (left) and Cool (right)

*T*he natural tones of our skin, hair and eyes will determine the colours that enhance us.

For many women, the colour 'temperature' of our features is the dominant determinant in terms of colour analysis.

If our features have a warm hue, warm colours suit us best. If we have a cool hue, cool colours are our palette.

Quick Test for Warm or Cool Undertones:

Place a white sheet of paper under the face in natural light and check for yellow or pink/blue undertones.

WARM SKIN TONES

OUR CATEGORY IS SPRING OR AUTUMN

Skin: Warm skin tones are yellow-based and evident in golden, olive or peachy skin. The skin can have a warm glow or subdued warmth. Warm skin is prone to freckles.

Eyes: Warm brown or hazel, olive green, warm blue.

Hair: Medium in intensity. Natural redheads from strawberry blonde to copper or deep auburn have warm undertones. Light to medium golden blondes often have warm skin tones as do brunettes with mid-brown hair with red highlights. Darker ethnicities can have hair with warm undertones. Blonde or light brown hair that acquires warm highlights in the sun is an indication of warm undertones.

Contrast between skin, hair and eyes: Medium. Skin exudes soft warm hues and so does hair and eyes.

Tell-tale signs: Warm skin tans easily and gold, orange, yellow and coral colours enhance warm skin tones.

I have warm skin, hair and eye tones, how do I know if I am Spring or Autumn?

Autumn women have warm undertones with red, chestnut or auburn hair and hazel, brown or green eyes.

Spring women have warm undertones with light hair and light eyes.

COOL SKIN TONES

OUR CATEGORY IS SUMMER OR WINTER

*S*kin: Cool skin tones have a pink, blue, grey or red-based tones rather than yellow, peachy undertones. Cool skin tends to appear rosy, porcelain, cool beige or pale.

Eyes: Violet, blue, blue-grey, steel grey, hazel, brown, black.

Hair: Silver ash blonde, silver grey, silver ash brown, dark brown, brown or black. Greyish or subdued brown or blonde tones. There are no warm highlights when exposed to sun.

Contrast between skin, hair and eyes: Medium to High. Skin may be pale compared to hair and eye colours.

Tell-tale signs: Cool skin is prone to burn, and it tans red rather than golden. Silver, blue, pinks and rich colours enhance cool skin tones.

I have cool skin, hair and eye tones, how do I know if I am Summer or Winter?

Summer women have cool undertones with light to medium ash hair and light to medium eyes

Winter women have cool undertones with dark or grey hair and dark or bright eyes.

LIGHT OR DEEP PROPERTIES

ARE THE COLOURS OF OUR FEATURES LIGHT OR DEEP?

Light features (left) and deep features (right)

*A*nother determinant in colour analysis is how light or dark our hair and eyes are compared to our skin.

The depth, especially of our hair colour, corresponds with the depth of the colours that enhance our beauty.

If our hair colour is darker, we are a Winter or an Autumn category.

If our natural hair colour is lighter to medium coloured, then we are usually typed as a Spring or Summer category.

LIGHT FEATURES

OUR CATEGORY IS SPRING OR SUMMER

*L*ight Skin: This skin colouring complements hair and eyes rather than contrasts with them.

Eyes: Light to medium in any colour depending on skin tone. For example, we are not light featured if we have brown eyes and light skin as the contrast is too strong.

Hair: Light to medium ash, golden blonde, light auburn, light to medium brown on darker-skinned ethnicities.

Contrast between skin, hair and eyes: All features are light and delicate, so contrast is low. Blue-eyed blondes are often light featured.

Tell-tale signs: Light shades enhance our look, while dark colours overwhelm us and catch the shadows under our eyes and around the mouth.

Whether we have cool or warm skin undertones, the hair and eye colours of the 'light' person are light and gentle and complement the light skin.

DEEP FEATURES

OUR CATEGORY IS AUTUMN OR WINTER

*D*eep Skin: This skin can be any colour from pale to dark skins once they contrast highly with hair and eyes.

Deep Eyes: Dark green, dark hazel, dark brown or black. In rare instances very dark blue.

Deep Hair: Very dark. Dark brown, dark auburn, black.

Contrast between skin, hair and eyes: Medium to high. Those with deep features have dark hair and dark eyes on a lighter skin tone.

Tell-tale signs: Dark, rich and vibrant colours enhance our eyes and hair while lighter shades fail to flatter the wearer or makes us look unwell.

Whether we have cool or warm skin undertones, the hair and eye colours of the 'deep' person are dark and saturated and contrast with the skin.

SOFT OR CLEAR FEATURES

ARE THE COLOURS OF OUR FEATURES SOFT OR CLEAR?

'Soft' muted green eyes (left) and 'Clear' bright blue eyes (Right)

The levels of colour saturation in our hair and eyes determines whether soft and muted OR bright and clear colours best suit our natural look.

SOFT & MUTED

OUR CATEGORY IS AUTUMN OR SUMMER

Clear and bright features.

*C*ontrast between skin, hair and eyes: Low. The overall look is soft and gentle.

Skin: Can be any colour but toned-down grey pigments are evident. The skin's warmth or coolness is not immediately evident.

Eyes: Indeterminate colours. Grey-blue, grey-green, hazel, soft brown.

Hair: Medium. Muted and subdued. Neither light nor dark. Softer browns and blondes with grey-out tones.

Tell-tale Signs: Muted, soft, dusky complementary colours add elegance to our look while vibrant colours swamp the soft-coloured person. Try a grey sheet of paper under the face and if the eyes appear grey-blue or grey green, the softer colour palettes of autumn or summer may suit.

CLEAR & BRIGHT

OUR CATEGORY IS SPRING OR WINTER

*C*ontrast between skin, hair and eyes: High. The hair and eyes contrast strongly with the skin.

Skin: Light or bright even for darker-skinned ethnicities. No grey pigmentation.

Eyes: Eyes may 'pop' against skin and hair. Bright blue eyes, turquoise, emerald, amber or bright brown eyes or deep brown or black.

Hair: White, bright blonde, medium brown to black.

Tell-tale signs: Bright or dark highly saturated shades and contrasting colours add vibrancy and life to the look of a 'clear' person. Soft tones with grey make the clear-coloured person look dull. The brighter palettes of Spring or Winter may suit.

THE TWELVE COLOUR CATEGORIES

*I*f we're born with flaming strawberry blonde hair and blue eyes for example, then it won't require Inspector Morse to work out that we are Warm Spring women.

And when we see grey-haired women with dark eyes, it's not hard to evaluate their colours as Cool Winter.

However, not everyone's colour category is so easy to work out. Some women's skin tones are quite neutral and it's difficult to decipher whether they fall into a 'cool' or 'warm' category.

And some women's eye colour and hair are muted so they know they belong to a 'soft' category but are they Soft Autumn or Soft Summer?

The following is an outline of all twelve colour categories, which may help us work out our perfect colour palette.

However, some of us may still require the expertise of good consultant with a mirror and her magic fabric drapes to discover our exact category!

NOTE ON EYE COLOUR:

Some women say they're not sure what colour eyes they have. They describe their eyes as indeterminate in colour, and they claim they look different in every light. If this is the case, they are usually like my eyes which are a shade of blue-grey. The beauty of these eyes is that they usually reflect the colours we wear. So, when I wear blue, they look blue. When I wear turquoise, my eyes look turquoise and when I wear green, they look green. People often envy those with very striking eyes like bright blue ones or chocolate brown ones, but they can never be chameleons like the rest of us!

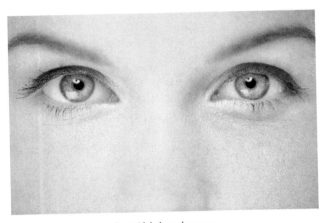

Beautiful chameleon eyes

LIGHT SPRING: LIGHT AND WARM

*Y*ou are light spring if your dominant characteristic is 'light' and your secondary trait is 'warm'.

Eye colour: Pale blue, pale green, light grey,

Hair colour: Golden blonde to lightest brown with warm gold going through it.

Skin tone: Light and warm; pale with creamy, peachy tones.

Colours: Light shades with warm hues. Light shades are all from the colourful spring palette but with white added. Delicate pastel colours look great. Colour contrast is low and for our best look, we wear colours that complement or are monochrome.

Business Colours: Beige, light sand, light grey, bright navy and cream.

Not Flattering: White, black, vivid colours or dark colours.

Celebrities: Scarlett Johansson, Goldie Hawn, Kirsten Dunst.

LIGHT SPRING MAKE UP COLOURS

Foundation: Yellow-based, golden-hued foundation.

Lipsticks: Light corals, Light peach, gentle nude-browns.

Eyes: Sand beige, creams, pale peach, pale coral, pale blue, pale green, lilac.

Eyeliner: Soft grey eyeliner. **Mascara**: Brown.

Blusher: Light coral or light peach.

WARM SPRING: WARM AND CLEAR

*Y*ou are warm spring if your dominant characteristic is warm colouring and your second is clear, vibrant look.

Eye colour: Medium light, bright and warm. Eyes colours are light green, grey, warm blue.

Hair colour: Strawberry blonde red hair and very warm golden tones with red hues.

Skin tone: Fair to dark with warm and golden undertones and often with freckles.

Colours: Warm, clear, bright. Warm spring require the warmest colour palette with warmer shades of blue and soft tropical shades.

Business Colours: Soft navy, warm chocolate brown, tan, camel and cream.

Not Flattering: Dark colours, cool colours and neutrals. Bright white or black look harsh on Warm Spring.

Celebrities: Sarah Ferguson, Julianne Moore, Nicole Kidman, Drew Barrymore.

WARM SPRING MAKEUP COLOURS

Foundation: Yellow-based, golden-hued foundation.

Lipsticks: Soft orange, nude browns.

Eyes: Browns, coral, peaches and creams, green, blue, lilac, mauve.

Eyeliner: Grey eyeliner with blue eyes, brown with brown eyes.
Mascara: Brown. **Blusher**: Coral and peach.

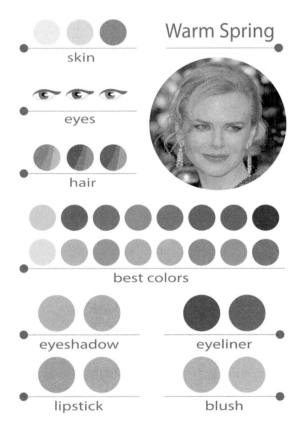

CLEAR SPRING: CLEAR AND WARM

*Y*ou are clear spring if your dominant characteristic is 'clear' and crisp and your secondary trait is 'warm' colouring.

Eye colour: Intense bright eyes in vibrant blue or bright green that stand out or contrast against skin and hair colour.

Hair colour: Mid to dark brown or black.

Skin tone: Fair to dark. More neutral. Clearer and brighter than Warm Spring but still with warm undertones.

Colours: Colourful and vibrant shades like bright coral and vibrant orange that combine clear colours and some warm hues. Slightly cooler than Warm Spring.

Business Colours: Black, dark grey, warm grey, navy, dark brown and soft white.

Not Flattering: Muted or dusty shades and quiet colours like grey, tan and beige.

Celebrities: Princess Caroline, Cara Delevingne, Katy Perry, Megan Fox.

CLEAR SPRING MAKEUP COLOURS

Foundation: Yellow-based, golden-hued foundation.

Lipsticks: Vivid coral pink or a bright red-orange lipstick like scarlet. **Eyes**: Bright peach, vibrant coral, gold, cream, bright green, bright blue. **Eyeliner**: Grey with blue eyes, brown with brown eyes. **Mascara**: Brown.

Blusher: Bright coral pink.

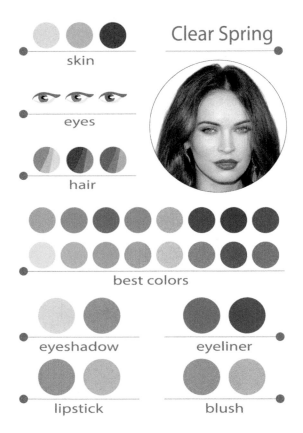

LIGHT SUMMER: LIGHT AND COOL

*Y*ou are Light Summer if your dominant characteristic is your light features and your secondary trait is a cool skin tone.

Eye colour: Light blue, pale green, pale grey

Hair colour: Light ash blonde to very light ash brown

Skin Tone: Cool, very light, blue and grey undertones, translucent skin which easily burns.

Colours: Softer and cooler than Light Spring. Not as vibrant. Red hues like pale raspberry, light pinks, greens and blue with cool hues. Dusty pastel colours with cool tones.

Business Colours: Silver grey, bright navy blue and chalk white.

Not Flattering: Bold colours, warm colours or very dark colours. Black and bright white are unflattering.

Celebrities: Gwyneth Paltrow, Reese Witherspoon, Saoirse Ronan.

Foundation: Cool or blue-based foundation with pink tones.

Lipsticks: Light pinks, baby pink, gentlest of pink shades.

Eyes: Pale grey, pastel pink, soft white, pale blue, pale green, lilac.
Eyeliner: Grey. **Mascara**: Navy or grey.

Blusher: Pastel pink. Barely-there nude blush.

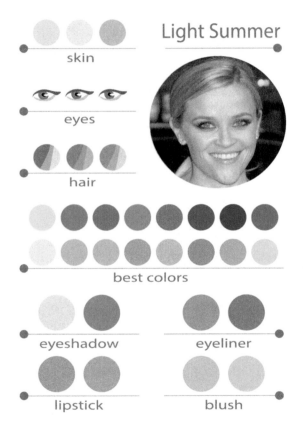

COOL SUMMER: COOL AND SOFT

$\mathcal{Y}$ou are Cool Summer if your dominant characteristic is a cool skin tone and your secondary characteristic is soft colouring in the hair and eyes.

Eye colour: Grey-blue, green, grey and hazel.

Hair colour: Grey, silver hair.

Skin tone: Cool tones in pink, porcelain and cool beige tones.

Colours: Soft, cool tones in darker pastels and mid-range colours of blues, greens, pinks. dark raspberry.

Business Colours: Mid-grey, charcoal, mole brown, navy, ivory white.

Not Flattering: Saturated or dark colours especially black and white. Warm colours like orange.

Celebrities: Queen Elizabeth, Helen Mirren.

Foundation: Cool or blue-based foundation with pink tones.
Lipsticks: Nude pinks, light pinks, bright pinks, raspberry red shades, medium plum.

Eyes: Grey, pink, white, silver, blue, green, mauve. **Eyeliner**: Grey.
Mascara: Navy or grey.

Blusher: Light to mid-pink.

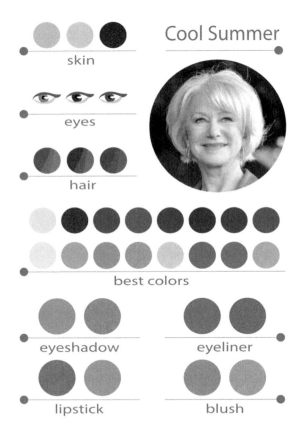

SOFT SUMMER: SOFT AND COOL

$\mathcal{Y}$ou are Soft Summer if your dominant characteristic is soft colouring in the hair and eyes and your secondary characteristic is a cool skin tone.

Eye colour: Soft blue-grey, green-grey eyes.

Hair colour: Muted. Medium ash-blonde, medium ash-brown or grey haired.

Skin tone: Cool, pink or ash tones.

Colours: Darkest in the summer family but still faded and powdery in blue, rose pink or soft, cool berry shades or wine red.

Business Colours: Mid-blues, navy, grey, mole brown, off-white.

Not Flattering: Harsh contrasts, electric colours, black, white or warm shades.

Celebrities: Jennifer Lawrence, Kate Moss, Kate Middleton, Jennifer Aniston, Taylor Swift, Khloe Kardashian, Ivanka Trump.

SOFT SUMMER MAKEUP COLOURS

Foundation: Cool or blue-based foundation with pink tones.

Lipsticks: Nude pink lipsticks, pale pinks, dusky-pinks, light plum.
Eyes: Soft greys, soft blues, soft green, white, silver. **Eyeliner**: Navy or grey. **Mascara**: Navy or grey.

Blusher: Soft dusky pink blushers.

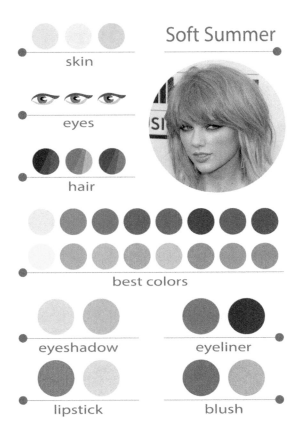

DEEP AUTUMN: DEEP AND WARM.

*Y*ou are Deep Autumn if your dominant characteristic is dark colouring in the hair and eyes and your secondary characteristic is a warm skin tone.

Eye colour: Warm dark brown, warm black-brown, dark hazel, green.

Hair colour: Dark auburn, dark chestnut, dark red, dark brown with a tendency to have red or golden highlights in summer.

Skin tone: Caramel, warm olive, golden beige. Warm tones in deep colouring. Lighter in winter. Freckles appear and tans easily in summer.

Colours: Dark, rich and warm tones with more vivid colours than other Autumn colourings. Teal green, dark pinks, orange, carmine red, maroon red.

Business colours: Dark warm browns, dark olive, navy with warm cream or off-white.

Not Flattering: Black, bright white or fully saturated colours that suit Winter colourings. Steer away from muted, soft or pastel colours.

Celebrities: Posh Spice, Susan Sarandon, Ariana Grande, Eva Longoria, Angela Bassett.

DEEP AUTUMN MAKEUP COLOURS

Foundation: Yellow-based, golden-hued foundation.

Lipsticks: Deep fire red or dark rust lipsticks, dark browns like terracotta. **Eyes**: Dark brown or dark green, mauve, cream or gold highlights. **Eyeliner**: Dark brown.

Mascara: Dark brown or black.

Blusher: Dark brown, brick or rust shades of blusher.

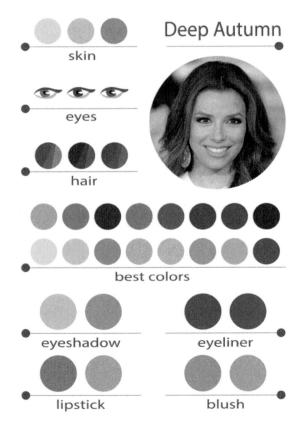

WARM AUTUMN: WARM AND SOFT

*Y*ou are Warm Autumn if your dominant characteristic is warm, golden colouring in the hair, eyes and skin and your secondary characteristic is soft, muted colours.

Eye colour: Brown or green, warm hazel, golden brown, warm olive green.

Hair colour: Medium to bright red hair colour. Light to mid auburn,

Skin tone: Medium cream to warm and golden or bronze. Prone to freckles and tans easily in summer,

Colours: Warm and golden shades with rich tones like cardinal red, orange, blue-green shades. Veers to darker end of colour scale.

Business Colours: Golden brown, bronze, mid-navy or deep olive.

Not Flattering: Cool blues, grey, lavender, lilac or any pastel shade. Black or bright white are too harsh.

Celebrities: Julianne Moore, Beyoncé Knowles, Debra Messing, Emma Stone.

Foundation: Yellow-based, golden-hued foundation

Lipsticks: Warm orange lipsticks, orange-based shades like tangerine, pumpkin colours, bronze

Eyes: Browns, warm beiges, green, blue, gold, cream highlighter. **Eyeliner**: Brown. **Mascara**: Brown. **Blusher**: Peach or nude-peach shades

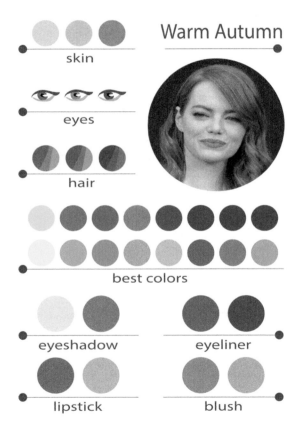

SOFT AUTUMN: SOFT AND WARM

*Y*ou are Soft Autumn if your dominant characteristic is soft, muted colouring in the eyes and hair and your secondary characteristic is a warm skin tone.

Eye colour: Muted brown, green or hazel.

Hair colour: Soft golden blonde or subdued mid-blonde or mid-brown with warm tones.

Skin tone: Warm tones of medium beige, olive or peachy skin. Prone to freckles in summer.

Colours: Rich but gentle shades of salmon, terracotta, coral, brick red, blue-greys, turquoise.

Business Colours: Taupe, soft navy, marine blue, camel, cream.

Not Flattering: Dark, cool and bright colours. Black or cool grey are not flattering. Pinks are best in coral pink shades.

Celebrities: Cindy Crawford, Julia Roberts, Melania Trump, Jennifer Lopez.

Foundation: Yellow-based, golden-hued foundation.

Lipsticks: soft orange like peach, light orange red, warm clay colours, mixed spice, light bronze.

Eyes: Soft brown, soft green, soft mauves. Cream highlighter. **Eyeliner**: Mid-brown.

Mascara: Brown. **Blusher**: Soft brown or soft peach.

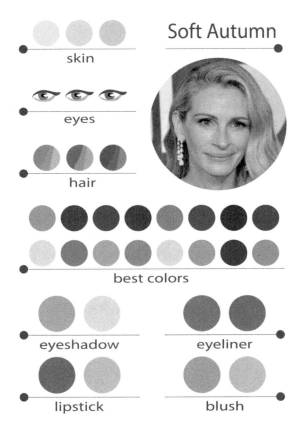

Soft Autumn

skin

eyes

hair

best colors

eyeshadow   eyeliner

lipstick   blush

DEEP WINTER: DEEP AND COOL

*Y*ou are Deep Winter if your dark features dominate and your secondary characteristic is a cool skin tone.

Eye colour: Dark eyes in black-brown, or dark hazel

Hair colour: Black, black-brown.

Skin tone: Cool and neutral skin with pink undertone or walnut brown or black skin.

Colours: Dark and intense or highly saturated. Deep reds with blue tones like claret red and cardinal red, purple, royal blue and deep green.

Business Colours: Black, dark navy, deep aubergine, deep burgundy, icy white.

Not Flattering: Warm pastels, soft colours, orange, warm yellow and warm browns.

Celebrities: Selena Gomez, Kamala Harris, Michelle Obama, Kim Kardashian, Meghan Markle.

Foundation: Cool blue-based foundation with pink tones. **Lipsticks**: Darker blue-based red lipsticks such as claret red, dark cardinal red, wine, dark fuchsia, deep cerise, dark magenta. **Eyes**: Charcoal, dark greys, silver, pink, dark blue, dark, green, deep mauve. White highlighter. **Eyeliner**: Black **Mascara**: Black. **Blusher**: Deep pink blusher.

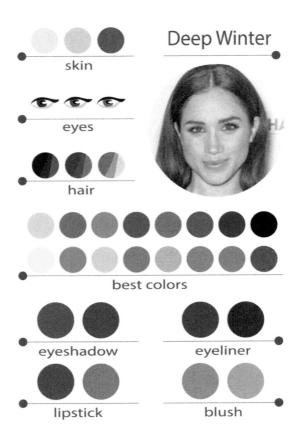

COOL WINTER: COOL AND CLEAR.

*Y*ou are Cool Winter if your cool blue undertones dominate your hair, skin and eyes and your secondary characteristics is the clear appearance of your features.

Eye colour: dark slate grey, cool dark brown

Hair colour: Silver or grey, platinum, salt-and-pepper colour

Skin tone: Cool, pink and porcelain to cool beige-brown.

Colours: Cool and clear with bright icy shades and vibrant shades like fuchsia or deep violet. Red in crimson or carmine red.

Business Colours: Inky black, dark navy, deep blue, mid-grey and icy white as contrast.

Not Flattering: Warm colours like oranges and corals, pastels or soft shades like lavender.

Celebrities: Glenn Close, Meryl Streep, Judy Dench, Diana Keaton, Ellie Goulding (with platinum hair), Lady Gaga.

Foundation: Cool blue-based foundation with pink tones.

Lipsticks: blue-based red lipsticks in mid-tones like rose-red, raspberry, magenta, fuchsia, cerise or plum.

Eyes: Mid-shades of grey, silver, pink, blue, green, mauve, white highlighter. **Eyeliner**: Grey, charcoal.

Mascara: Black. **Blusher**: Mid-pink blusher.

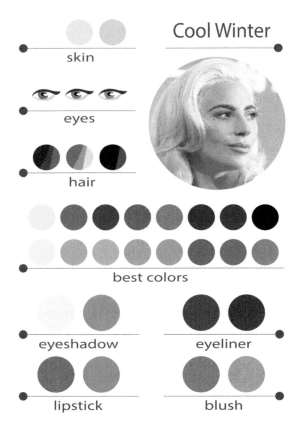

CLEAR WINTER: CLEAR AND COOL

*Y*ou are a Clear Winter if your clear bright skin, eyes and hair dominate, and your secondary characteristic is your cool colouring.

Eye colour: Bright blue, vivid green eyes or bright brown/amber eyes.

Hair colour: Black, dark brown.

Skin tone: Clear porcelain or pink tones that easily burn. Skin tends to be very white or very light for our ethnicity and eyes are bright and contrasting.

Colours: Vivid and clear with shades like hot pink, electric purple and azure blue or jewel shades like amethyst, ruby red, true red or emerald.

Business Colours: Black, silver grey, navy, bright white.

Not Flattering: Warm colours like orange, coral and soft colours like dusty pink and lilac.

Celebrities: Andrea Corr, Eve Hewson, Catherine Zeta Jones, Rihanna, Courtney Cox.

CLEAR WINTER MAKEUP COLOURS

Foundation: Cool blue-based foundation with pink tones.

Lipsticks: blue-based clear lipsticks like bright cherry red, crimson, vibrant raspberry or bright cerise.

Eyes: Silver grey and light pinks. Bright blue or green. White as a highlighter.

Eyeliner: Charcoal.

Mascara: Black.

Blusher: Bright pink blusher, nude pinks.

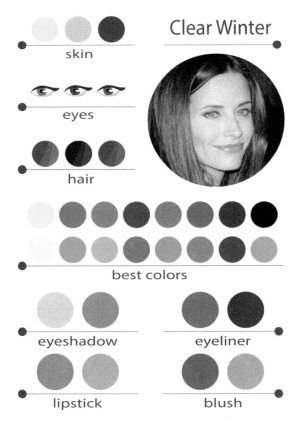

BEST LIPSTICKS FOR YOUR CATEGORY

Deep Winter   Clear Winter   Cool Winter

Light Summer   Soft Summer   Cool Summer

Deep Autumn   Soft Autumn   Warm Autumn

Light Spring   Clear Spring   Warm Spring

The Colour Analysis Consultation

*A*s a veteran colour consultant of thirty-five years, I can usually tell a person's colour palette as they walk through the door.

The trick is often convincing the client that they don't really have sallow skin or that their favourite colour in the world (usually black) is overpowering their beautiful, light colouring.

I usually ask clients to arrive wearing their usual make-up so I can assess what they use and if it works for their skin colouring. Then we remove the make-up so that we can assess their skin tones accurately.

Colour analysis is about discovering the exact palette of colour that enhances our skin tone, our eye colour and our hair colour.

We start, as usual, by ascertaining whether the undertones of our skin, hair and eyes are warm or cool. We also look at how light or deep our overall colouring is - paying attention to the natural colour of our hair or how muted or clear our colouring is.

However, if the client dyes their hair for example, it's not always immediately apparent which of the cooler categories Winter and Summer or the warmer ones Spring or Autumn they belong to.

This is where the real magic begins. In front of a mirror, I drape large fabric swatches from different categories across the client. She or he rarely needs me to say anymore because they can see instantly what is happening to their faces.

When the right colour palette is draped on a person, they look fresh and energised. When the incorrect colour palette is used, they look tired and the dark shadows under their eyes and around the mouths are accentuated.

Most people often cannot believe the transformation that takes place in front of their eyes as the colours are swapped and switched. They are left with no doubt about the colour palette that suits them.

Is she a Cool Summer or a Light Summer or a Soft Summer? Is she a Deep Autumn, a Warm Autumn or a Soft Autumn? Simply draping the fabrics under their faces will tell.

They can see the transformation in front of their eyes. It really is like magic!

HAIR DYE DISASTERS

I have lost count of the times I have seen a woman walk into the room with the most beautiful tumbling red locks or golden blonde hair. Then I see her complexion, and it's cool in tone, pink in hue and clashes dreadfully with her hair colour. Her hair may be wonderful, but it is wearing her, not the other way around.

People's eye and skin colouring usually remains as God made them, but many of the people who come to me colour their hair. And there is nothing wrong at all with colouring our hair, but it's just far better to work with our natural colouring rather than fight it.

The Duchess of Cambridge, Kate Middleton, is a green-eyed Soft Summer who dyes her hair auburn. For her hair and skin combination to work well, she applies a lot of tan, so that she looks more of a Warm Autumn.

I know hairstylists and especially colourists who love the concept of colour analysis and understand about working with their clients' complexions. But I know other hairdressers who hear my recommendations and raise their eyes to heaven.

'What does she know about hairdressing?' they ask.

I am the first to admit that I know nothing about hairdressing. But I do understand skin tones, eye colour and hair colour. That's my forte, and women with cool pink complexions and pink blush in their cheeks are not complementing their natural looks by going into a hair salon and coming out with glossy red hair.

Many hairdressers recommend lightening hair in the summer when their clients' complexions are at their darkest and most tanned. It's only when the skin lightens, that I recommend lightening the hair. Our skin always lightens in the winter, so lighter make-up colours and a lighter hair shade works best in the darkest months of the year rather than in the summer.

When we have cool pink skin, our hair colour looks best with ash tones and pearl tones.

When we have warm, peachy skin with freckles and a yellow under-tone, any hair colour with golden or red tones will work beautifully.

Our skin colour and our eyes are the two constants in our life. So, when we change our hair colour and our clothes, I always recommend that we honour our skin and our eye tone by using complementary colours. It's all about harmony. There is no point in having beautiful hair if it doesn't look well on us!

FADE TO GREY

I've met many people who believe that there's a golden rule that our hair colour has to go lighter as we grow older. And there are many hairstylists who steer their older clients into fairer and blonder colours as they age.

Yet women like Joan Collins and Elizabeth Taylor kept their hair dark and lustrous looking throughout their lives and always looked wonderful.

Other women choose to let their hair go grey as they get older. It can be a great freedom not to have to colour our hair and touch-up our roots anymore.

Just remember that when we go grey or silver, our hair becomes our dominant feature.

Grey and silver are cool colours, so I always recommend adjusting our colour palettes accordingly.

Silver-haired women with brown or black eyes become Cool Winter. Meanwhile, those with blue or green eyes become Cool Summer.

Grey-haired people look better when they steer away from muted or warmer colours. Their look is enhanced by more vivid, saturated colours which add vitality to their hair, skin and eyes.

With the right, bright colours and lipstick, the grey-haired mature woman's eyes and skin can 'pop'.

One of my friends went grey, shaped her hair into a smart bob, wears all the right cool winter colours and she looks amazing.

When she wears the colours that flatter her look, the silver-haired woman never fades to grey.

THE BLACK MAGIC MYTH

If I have one bugbear, it would be Irish women's devotion to wearing black! So many women make black their winter wardrobe staple and remain convinced by all these fashion myths about the colour being 'timeless' and 'classic' and 'slimming'.

Lots of clients tell me that most of their wardrobe is black, and they are unwilling to change. But as soon I do the 'magic' with the fabric drapes and the mirror, they understand why I recommend they stay away from the colour.

Unfortunately, black is a difficult colour to wear. For many, the colour only serves to enhance the black circles under their eyes and the lines on their faces. It drains most complexions. Black is also a colour that is even harder to wear as we grow older. Only those with Winter colouring can carry off black with real style.

Even then, I believe most Winter women look even better wearing sapphire blue or emerald green, which highlights their brilliant blue eyes or makes their green eyes pop!

Black doesn't even suit a lot of Winter people after a certain age especially if they wear it close to the face.

Of course, black can look smart and powerful as a neutral colour for the business wardrobe. However, it's not the best colour if our job entails a lot of interaction and negotiation with colleagues and clients.

Black is a stern, forbidding colour, which has an aura of authority and menace about it. It was no accident that black was adopted by the Nazi party for their SS paramilitary uniforms.

It is also no accident that black is also used as the uniform of the clergy. It is 'stand-offish'. As a colour, it also has strong associations with power and control rather than collaboration and cooperation.

I often suggest dark navy or deep aubergine as neutral colours for business as they are less intimidating and, often, more flattering on Winter skins. Also, eye contact is important in business, so when a blue-eyed person wears blue for example, it reflects on the eye and makes them appear brighter, more vital and friendly.

By wearing black, it places an automatic barrier between us and other people.

So, remember, before we go back to black, it's not always as bewitching a colour as we think!

The Value of Neutrals

Years ago, I bought a beautiful, bright purple coat in Blarney Woollen Mills. Oh, how I loved that coat!

Up until then I wore a good, black wool coat every winter with lots of bright accessories in my colour palette. It cost a lot of money, so it was an investment piece, and I wore it for about a decade.

The black coat was shoved into the back of the wardrobe as soon as I bought the purple coat. The shade of purple really was my colour, and I felt good in it. I wore it every day going to work that winter.

The following year, I took out the black coat, and I took out the purple coat, and there was no contest. I still loved the purple coat, so I chose to wear it again that winter.

A few days later, I remember meeting an acquaintance in town. She looked me up and down and said, 'Jesus, Marion, you live in that purple coat.'

I wore my black coat for a decade, and nobody ever said that to me once. That remark was pretty much the beginning of the end of the purple coat.

If she said it to me now, I wouldn't give a hoot. But in those days, it mattered to me as an image consultant that I wasn't seen in the same clothes all the time.

The problem was that once someone saw that coat, they remembered it. They retained the colour in their heads. So, it was probably a wonderful colour to wear for a business appointment or a first date if I wanted to be remembered. But as a workday coat, the neutral black one was the most useful garment, and it continued to be a stylish essential in my wardrobe for years.

I always recommend that the more an item of clothing costs, the more useful, versatile and classic it needs to be.

When we spend a lot of money on clothes – for a coat, suit, evening dress or wedding outfit - it is better to buying them in neutral colours such as beige, black, grey or navy. That way, the garment earns its keep by being adaptable and flexible and lasting for years.

For business, I usually recommend neutral colours as the base colour for suits and then suggest using accent colours from our colour palettes for shirts or scarves.

Whenever I'm tempted by a bright colour with an expensive price tag, I think of that purple coat, and I put it back on the rail!

PART IV
THE PSYCHOLOGY OF COLOURS

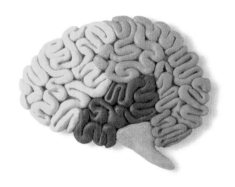

THE PSYCHOLOGY OF COLOURS

*D*o we feel calmer and more relaxed in a green room? Do we feel anxious around red? Many believe that colours can alter our emotions and moods. Some studies have shown that some colours are associated with increased blood pressure, raising appetite or increasing feelings of hostility.

I know that when I apply a good orange-hued red lipstick, I feel ready to take on the world. I surround myself in turquoise blue in my home, because I feel happier and relaxed around it.

All colours are associated with an emotional experience, so it's possible to use the colour in situations where we are trying to persuade.

The fast-food chain, McDonald's, use red and yellow as their theme colours because they believe red urges us to eat faster and studies of yellow have shown it can stimulate hunger.

Similarly, we can use shades of green and blue in the business environment to relax people or to tell them we are environmentally friendly. We can use red or bright orange to provoke people into action like buying.

Choosing the colours for our home, our wardrobe, our business or our office can be an important consideration.

In the business context, wearing colours that enhance the colour of our eyes makes the businesswoman look more striking and enhances eye contact.

BLUE

Blue is a colour of nature, evoking calming feelings of sky and water so it is excellent to use in the business environment and our wardrobe.

- People usually associate blue with serene and calm surroundings. Baby blue, light blue, powder blue, lavender blue, turquoise and azure are soft and calming ends of the colour scale.
- It is a good colour for the workplace in any creative field as it is said to be inspiring.
- Some studies have shown that people work more productively in blue surroundings.
- It is a good colour for business because it is non-threatening and is often said to evoke feelings of sincerity, stability, reliability, maturity, spirituality and security.
- If our job requires connecting with people and appearing trustworthy, a blue suit is an appropriate colour, especially

if we have blue eyes. Or wearing bright blue or turquoise as an accent colour under navy or grey can also look effective in the business environment.

- Blue will mean that we are taken seriously in business.

Red makes us think of a myriad of things including blood, love hearts and red roses, the red cloak of the matador and the 'stop!' signs on the road. Red is great as an accent colour with a dark suit for extra energy. I'd wear a red top at work if I was tired or a bit lethargic any day

and it gives me a lift. In evening wear, red is glorious for women.

I know a woman who works in an all-male environment, and she says she wears red a lot at work. 'Why do you wear red?' I asked.

'So, I stand out from all the men.'

'Surely, being the only woman, you stand out from the men?' I said. But red is also quite an intimidating colour, so she feels more in charge when she wears it. It's best worn with caution in the business situation unless, of course, our intention is to intimidate!

- Red is a statement colour that draws all eyes and adds great energy to our look, but in a collaborative or caring work environment, it is a colour that can be aggressive and overpowering.

- Red is the boldest colour of all and has connotations of passion, danger, excitement and anger.
- It also prompts feelings of heat and warmth and danger because it's associated with fire.
- Being highly visible, it's often used to convey danger. It can also provoke aggression and so we have the expression that someone is 'seeing red'.
- It is a colour of dominance, power and strength so it's probably no accident that some of the best teams in football like Liverpool, Manchester United, Arsenal, Bayern Munich and AC Milan tog out in red. Or that Donald Trump has always liked to wear red ties. Cardinals, the leaders of the Catholic church, wear red too.
- Some studies have even shown that being exposed to red results in an increased heart rate and raised blood pressure levels.
- It is used as a colour in the business world to promote urgency, speed and impulse buying.
- It's not advised as a colour to wear in a collaborative or caring work environment like a hospital, medical clinic or a school.

ORANGE

Orange is a blend of the warmth of red and the joy of yellow so it's a colour that communicates fun and playfulness. There are so many shades of orange from bright tangerine and marigold to pumpkin, burnt orange and coral to softer hues like peach and apricot and salmon.

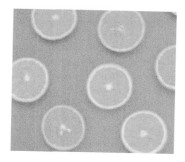

- The more vibrant shades can be seen as more stimulating and aggressive. Mid-hues can be more about creativity and enthusiasm.
- Softer hues of orange have connotations of cheerfulness, affordability and frivolity.
- It can be seen as energising in the business context and make help provoke impulse buying.
- Orange is a good-natured colour overall. It has an energetic punch that encourages social interaction and friendly stimulation.

- It's a great accent colour for blouse or T-shirt to be worn under a suit.

GREEN

Green is the colour of nature, of
trees, lush grass and plants and wide,
open spaces in the countryside. It
evokes concepts like health, rest,
nature, growth and relaxation.

- It's a good refreshing and
  relaxing colour for business
  surroundings, especially those
  in the caring, environmental
  and pampering businesses.
- Because it's linked to growth it's also often associated with
  financial businesses.
- Most shades of blue and green walls will work in business
  and private situations where we want the atmosphere to be
  serene and relaxed.
- Green-eyed people look wonderful wearing green and the
  colour inspires feelings of reliability, safety, honesty and
  harmony.
- Suits and separates in soft or deep green are striking or tops

worn as accent colours in shades of green with navy, grey or beige look appealing too.

- Green is a reassuring colour in the business environment

PINK

Pink is a colour that evokes romance, femininity and luxurious-ness. It is good colour in a work environment where there is a context of softness and vulnerability.

- When working with older people and young children for example, pink is a nice soft colour for our surroundings. Gentler shades of pink may also be a good addition to our wardrobe when we work in those caring environments.
- In a normal business environment, pink can be a little too soft. It is not a serious colour or a shade that will inspire confidence in a bank manager or a doctor for example.
- It's more of a fun, frivolous colour especially in the more vivid shades of pink like bubble gum and candy pink.
- Fuchsia pink is often a good statement colour as it blends purple, pink and red, but sends out a message that says, 'Look at me!'

BLACK

Black is a colour that I've already written about at length. I will repeat, however, that it is not a flattering colour for most women apart from those who belong to the Winter category.

- Black is a difficult colour to wear and highlights dark circles and lines on our faces.
- It is also not a great colour for the business suit because it is a stern and forbidding colour which has associations with power and control rather than teamwork or cooperation.
- By wearing black, it places an automatic barrier between us and other people.
- However, black will work in senior management for women who prefer an authoritative management style because it is a colour that evokes power, formality and seriousness.
- Many famous brands use black in their logos and marketing because black is also associated with luxuriousness, sensuality and masculinity.

- Women who work in a persuasive, participative or collaborative working environments like sales or coaching are advised to wear a colour like navy which has less of a hard edge.

YELLOW

Yellow is a lovely airy colour that makes us feel energetic and upbeat. In the business environment, it exudes cheer, youthful energy and friendliness.

- It is good for a busy and youthful office environment as it is stimulating.
- Beware, however, too much and too bright a yellow can cause anxiety and agitation especially in an environment which is already stressful.
- Yellow is not a colour to be worn head to toe in a business context, but it makes a cheerful accent colour to lift a sober navy, grey, nude or taupe suit if it's the right shade of yellow. It's a lovely addition to our wardrobe in the summer
- As a colour it imbues energy and optimism in the workplace.

BROWN

Brown is an earthy colour that also exudes a certain ruggedness and masculinity. It is a colour that is also associated with seriousness and reassurance, but it's not one that I associate with business wear. It's more for relaxed and casual wear.

- Chocolate brown seating and dark brown wooden floors add a sense of warmth, relaxation and solidity to any working environment.
- Brown is also a good for brown-eyed autumn women and works well in a casual setting with shirts and tops with accent colours of cream, off-white, orange and green.
- As a colour, it imbues feelings of confidence and reliability but is suitable in a relaxed setting rather than an office setting.

WHITE

White is the colour of any clinic, scientific and medical environment because it exudes cleanliness, sterility and purity.

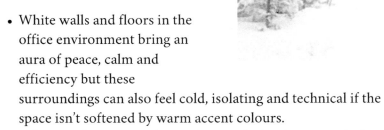

- White walls and floors in the office environment bring an aura of peace, calm and efficiency but these surroundings can also feel cold, isolating and technical if the space isn't softened by warm accent colours.
- White is often a secondary colour in the business wardrobe and a crisp white or off-white shirt is a staple of the classic office executive look where it contrasts with dark neutrals like black, navy, grey and beige.
- As a colour, white imbues efficiency, calm and reassurance in the workplace.

GREY

Grey is a blend of black and white without the starkness of either. It is an unemotional colour and has mature, classic and serious shades that are suitable for most office environments.

- It is a great neutral for the working woman's wardrobe because it is subdued and calm.
- Dark grey adds more mystery and formality to the look while lighter or silver grey is more accessible.
- It is considered a conservative and traditional colour which is excellent in some business environments.
- Sometimes, in its mid-hues, it can be regarded as dull and uninteresting but can be livened up with contrasting accent colours in blue, purple or red.
- Grey imbues feelings of stability, composure, tradition and reserve.

PURPLE

Purple is a rich, statement colour which exudes nobility, royalty, elegance, and sophistication. Purple is one of my favourite colours and is a great alternative to black especially in the context of evening wear.

- Purple has some of the 'look at me' vibrancy of red blended with the serenity and grace of blue.
- It's not a colour found in nature, so it stands out in the normal business context and is a great shade for anyone who needs to be seen – such as women in sales.
- It is also suited to more creative and artistic business environments where it exudes luxury, mystery and sensuality.
- Purple is also a great accent colour in a shirt, blouse or camisole as it can lift a grey suit or a navy, black or taupe one.
- Purple exudes a lot of glamour and confidence and it is little

surprise that it is the colour favoured by the bishops in the upper ranks of the Catholic and Anglican clergy.

PART V
THE BEAUTIFUL BODY
MAKEOVER

MARION'S BEAUTIFUL BODY
MAKEOVER

We are all unique people, with different bodies, tastes, lifestyles and with our own unique sense of style.

And if we're happy with everything in our wardrobe and we know what suits us, that's great! If we never make mistakes when we're shopping, well done!

However, if you have lots of clothes in the wardrobe with the price tags still attached, maybe read on.

And read on too if you ever wondered why you don't shine in the same coat style, which looks great on your friend.

For years before I was trained about my body shape, for example, I wondered why a business suit never looked right or felt comfortable on me. Learning about my body shape made me understand that the structured suit does not enhance me.

. . .

Once we understand our body lines and our face shapes, it makes shopping, going to the hairdressers, buying glasses and getting dressed in the morning so much easier!

Before we begin, do the following pages provide the definitive answers to all our fashion questions? No, they don't.

And do we have to stick rigidly to all these style and image rules? Not at all!

As with everything in this book, what follows is a general guide. There is no rulebook. These are recommendations, suggestions and general tips which I have learnt and gathered over years of working in the fashion and image consultancy business.

However, it's you, and you alone who decides what feels and look right for you because ultimately, your body and your shape are unique to you.

So, if you love certain styles and you have garments in your wardrobe that bring you joy, then wear them with pride and enjoyment!

Nothing is banned, nothing is restricted, and everything is only recommended. The hope is that some of this guidance resonates with you, the reader, and makes life easier, the shopping experience simpler and ultimately saves you money, time and effort!

The section contains suggestions (only suggestions!) that can help us look and feel our absolute best. The aim is to provide a guide that can help us be our happiest and most confident selves.

For me, these are the final secrets that allow us to unwrap the beauty that lies within ourselves and which makes life simpler for us too!

THE FIVE FANTASTIC FACE SHAPES

Let's start from the premise that our face shape is always perfect for *us*.

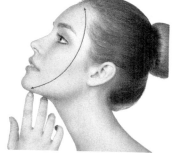

Whatever our face shape, it's our beautiful face and our beautiful shape and if we are happy with our hair and makeup, that's great!

The following are only my suggestions for the kind of hair styles and makeup that I believe best complement each different face shapes.

Once we identify our face shape, it can help us choose the hairstyle and makeup that complements our features.

The idea is to learn how to flatter our face shape by tailoring our hair and makeup - and even our glasses and sunglasses to suit our look.

Once we understand face shapes, we can be more confident in the hair salon. We can also apply contour and blush with confidence if we use them.

Many of the most celebrated and beautiful women in the world have oblong, square, round and heart-shaped faces. However, multiple studies have shown that the oval shape face is regarded as the most symmetrical and that symmetrical faces are considered attractive in both men and women.

If we want to add symmetry and definition to our faces, my suggestion is to choose hairstyles and apply makeup that give the *illusion* of the oval face.

For example, for those with a square-shaped face with its typically strong jawline, I usually suggest choosing a hairstyle and makeup that softens the jaw.

And for those with an oblong face, I recommend choosing hair and makeup that have the illusion of shortening the elongated shape.

There are five basic face shapes although sometimes our face shape will lean towards a combination of two shapes.

Remember, weight gain can very easily change our natural shape into a round. I am a natural oval shape, but I've been more round recently. But now that I am losing weight in Slimming World, my natural oval shape is returning!

WHAT IS MY FACE SHAPE?

*L*ooking straight into a mirror, pull all your hair back from your face and secure it. Pin back your fringe too if you have one until you can see the whole outline of your face.

Some people advocate taking a fabric tape measure and measuring the forehead, cheekbones, jawline and face length to determine the longest, widest and narrowest parts of the face.

However, most of us can determine the shape of our faces easily if we focus on the outline and all the angles and curves.

Note where your face is at its widest – is it the forehead, cheekbones or jawline?

Note the length of your face relative to the width.

Look at which parts of your face are the narrowest – forehead, cheekbones or jawline?

Is your chin pointy, square or round?

Note About Blush

Remember when applying blush or contour, dust off the excess before applying so that you get a light dusting rather than a streak or blob of colour.

Regarding Glasses

These days I'm wearing turquoise-rimmed glasses, and people tend to remark on them a lot. They stand out, and they are more memorable as a result. I had gold-rimmed glasses, and no one ever remarked on them.

If we want glasses that we won't tire of after six or twelve months, we look for classic gold or silver frames. They will last for years and will complement our skin tones.

Go for gold-toned frames if you are a spring or autumn colour or silver ones if you are winter or summer.

If we want coloured frames, cooler skins can go for pink tones or look for rims that match the colours of our eyes or our hair colour. Warmer skins can go for peach or beige tones or match the colours of their eyes or hair colour.

Above all, remember the small woman looks best in smaller frames and the larger frames sizes will suit the larger woman.

THE OVAL SHAPE FACE

The Shape:

The oval-shaped face is regarded as the most symmetrical. Being oval means our face is longer than it is wide. Our jawline and chin are rounded rather than sharp and are narrower than the forehead.

Oval Makeup:

Makeup and shading are standard and subtle. Blush or bronzer is stroked gently inwards from the temples to the apples of the cheeks. The idea is to highlight the cheek bones. For additional highlighting, apply to the temples, brow bone, bridge of the nose and chin.

Oval face shape: Beyoncé Knowles

Oval Hair:

Those with an oval-shaped face are deemed to have a very balanced look so they can pretty much do what they like with their hair. The fuller hair looks are always attractive on the oval shape. Textured and layered cuts are also flattering, and those with a high forehead look good with a fringe.

Long or short, the oval face-shape can wear it all.

Oval Sunglasses/Glasses:

The oval-shaped face is balanced and symmetrical so can look good in most frames. Try frames that are as wide or wider than the broadest part of the face to keep the look balanced. Go for lenses and frames that are softly rounded.

Oval Celebrities:

Duchess of Cambridge Kate Middleton, Beyoncé, Angelina Jolie, Kim Kardashian.

Glasses for oval face shape.

THE SQUARE SHAPE FACE

The Shape:

If the length and width of the face are similar in measurement and there is a strong jawline, this indicates a square-shaped face. The forehead and jawline tend to be roughly the same width, and the jawline is squared and defined. The chin is not pointed.

Square Makeup:

Soften the edges of the face by adding contouring to the jawline and to the top corners of the forehead and temples. Use blush on the

Square face shape: Kelly Osbourne

apple of the cheek for a rounder, softer look. Add highlighter to the forehead and chin to add height. Bright lip colours or rounded smoky eyes also add the illusion of softness.

Square Hair:

This shaped face requires height, length and softness. The best look is anything with soft lift and height at the roots and a length that reaches to the shoulder. If the neck is long and slender, the hair can reach the shoulder blades or longer.

The least suitable style is a sharp, angular bob that ends at the jaw - the square-shaped face is wide on the jaw and it widens the face even further at that point.

Jennifer Aniston's soft and face-framing 'Rachel' cut which is feathered, layered and shoulder length is a good look.

Square Sunglasses/Glasses:

Soften the angles by steering away from square frames. Go for frames with oval or round shapes. Try adding height to the face by wearing frames that are wider than they are deep.

Glasses for square face shape.

Square Celebrities:

Cameron Diaz, Katie Holmes, Kelly Osborne, Sandra Bullock.

THE HEART SHAPE FACE

The Shape:

This face is often described as the 'inverted triangle' because the fore-head and cheekbones are a similar width and there is a strong jawline that comes into the chin in a point. The hairline sometimes has a 'V' or 'a widow's peak' in the middle of the forehead.

Heart Makeup:

Soften the top-heavy look by contouring in bronze or foundation along both sides of the forehead and the temples and just a tip on the end of the chin.

Heart shape face: Cheryl Cole

Focus blush on the apples of the cheeks for a softer shape. Highlight the bridge of the nose and Cupid's bow.

Draw attention away from the jawline with bright, glossy lips.

Heart Hair:

This face shape is perfect for a short bob because this widens the narrowest part of the face – the chin.

Sweeping side fringes also give the illusion of narrowing the forehead.

Top heavy haircuts which are very full on top or at the sides and accentuate the widest part of the face are not complementary.

Look for width and fullness in a hair style from the ear down only. Longer hair is best layered to frame the side of the face.

Heart Sunglasses/Glasses:

Light frames or rimless ones that have a less solid appearance are better on heart-shaped faces. Aviator frames or oval glasses are generally good. Go for frames that look wider on the bottom if possible.

Glasses for heart face shape.

Heart Celebrities:

Reese Witherspoon, Halle Berry, Cheryl Cole.

THE ROUND SHAPE FACE

The Shape:

If the widest part of the face is at the cheekbones, this often indicates a round-shaped face. The width of the cheekbones and the length of the face is usually similar. The width of the forehead and jawline is also similar but shorter in measurement than the width of the cheekbones.

Round shape face: Selena Gomez

A round-shaped face can be confused with the square-shaped one as the face length and width is the same. However, the jawline is soft and rounded and not defined.

Round Makeup:

Apply blush as angular as possible, in long dark strokes down the cheeks to make the face appear longer. We can also contour the hollow of our cheeks with dark foundation to make the face appear more oval. Bronze or contour the outer parts of the face – left and right at the forehead and temples and down to the jawline. Add highlighter to the forehead, cheekbones and chin to add

height and definition. Eyebrows look best as angled arches rather than round ones.

Round Hair:

This face shape looks at its best with hair which has some height and length to give the illusion of a more oval face. It's best not to go for volume on the sides as big, full hair accentuates the width of the face. We can wear it very short if the sides are narrow and the top has volume and lift. Long, sleek or layered hair to the shoulders and beyond is flattering. Short, curly hair will accentuate roundness.

Round Sunglasses/Glasses:

Add angles and straight lines to add definition to the face. Try rectangular, narrow eyeglass frames to lengthen the face. Frameless or rimless glasses suit the round-shaped face.

Round Celebrities:

Glasses for round face shape.

Mila Kunis, Adele, Selena Gomez, Oprah, Rebel Wilson, Melissa McCarthy.

THE OBLONG SHAPE FACE

The Shape:

Sometimes described as a long or 'rectangular' shape, the length of the face is the most obvious feature with the oblong shape. The forehead, cheekbones and jawline are often similar in width and always shorter in diameter than the length of the face.

Oblong Makeup:

Blush is best applied circled inwards across from the apple of the cheeks to the ear to add the illusion of width. Bronzer or contour is applied

Oblong shape face: Sarah Jessica Parker

at the hairline at the top of the forehead and under the chin up along the jawline to reduce height.

Highlight the tops of the cheek bones to the temples to add width. Try not to apply highlighter on the forehead or the chin as it adds length.

Oblong Hair:

The hairstyle which best suits this face shape is one which doesn't fall below the chin. Layers, a long fringe, and voluminous width in the hair are best for this face. Big, full wide hair is very flattering to the oblong face whereas longer hair drags and gives the illusion of lengthening the face further. For those who prefer longer cuts, they can opt for lots of layers and a fringe and keep the shade fluid, soft and full.

Oblong Sunglasses/Glasses:

Go for frames that are round or square or have at least as much depth as width to give the illusion of a shorter face. Wayfarers are often suitable. Frames with large or contrasting-coloured arms or decorations on the arms can also add width to the face.

Glasses for oblong shape face.

Oblong Celebrities:

Jennifer Anniston, Iman, Sarah Jessica Parker, Liv Tyler, Meryl Streep.

EXTRA MAKEOVER NOTES

*N*ail Polish:

To help nail polish last longer, apply it last thing at night and let it dry properly overnight. Any nail polish can be touch dry in minutes, but it really takes hours for it to harden properly.

Doing the dishes or having a shower in hot water after applying nail polish will reduce the life of our manicure because the heat causes the nail bed to expand, cracking the polish. Beware of the super-quick drying polishes, which are often full of alcohol and other harsh ingredients that weaken our nails.

229

I'd always recommend using gel nail polishes because they will normally last a week. Sally Hanson and Maybelline have good value home gel polishes that don't require UV lights to dry them. Apply two coats of gel nail polish and a top coat. Working women are best sticking to nude and pale colours only. For evenings or more casual wear, then bright colours for nails are fine.

Moisturiser:

Some women spend a lot of money on expensive moisturisers and creams, and that's okay. But I find it easy to protect my skin from wrinkles and dehydration, using serum, sun block and drinking water.

The skin's youthful appearance is affected more by exposure to the sun and smoking than by anything else. Instead of spending a lot on a moisturiser during the day, I go for a good sunblock. I like a good serum and an SPF 50 sun cream to protect the skin on my face during the day. I use a rich moisturiser at night.

Our skin is made from cells and cells are made up of water, so we need to stay hydrated for our skin to look and feel its best. Being well-hydrated also improves the circulation and digestion. When I remember to drink a lot of water, I find I eat less too and that it reduces sugar cravings. Win-win!

Head Health:

For my head health, I need to get outdoors, switch off the phone, get offline and connect with nature. Massages, yoga and acupuncture are great but connecting with nature is the easiest and cheapest way to feel physically and mentally healthier. It's the best way to be gentle and easy with myself, and to reduce anxiety and lessen stress.

I'm lucky where I live, I can get out on the winding country roads and rarely see a car. And I meditate as I walk. I say the rosary, and I connect with nature.

I always recommend that my clients find a park, a beach, a forest, a field, a garden or a body of water, somewhere to listen to the birds singing, the leaves rustling or just the wind blowing and get away from it all. Sit quietly or walk silently and bask in the sounds of nature.

The weather doesn't matter, in fact the wilder, the windier and wetter it is, the more we feel alive sometimes. Being out in nature is the best tonic for my mind and soul.

HOW TO DRESS FOR OUR HEIGHT

Dressing for our height is all about proportion. Let's say that we have to decorate a small room in our house. We're not going to place a big painting or a huge sofa in there because it will overwhelm the room and obstruct the space.

Also, we're also not going to decorate the small room using huge patterned wallpaper, curtains or carpet because we're going to make the space look even smaller.

And let's say we have a medium-sized or big room in our house to decorate. There's no point in hanging a tiny painting on the wall, no matter how exquisite it is, because it will be lost and make the space look bigger and badly proportioned.

It's similar when it comes to dressing and accessorising ourselves. We must dress to proportion to flatter our wonderful height. When we dress and accessorise proportionately to our size, the smaller woman won't be swamped by what she wears, and the larger woman will look balanced and proportionate.

Dressing the Small Woman
The Small Woman: 160cm or under/ 5ft 3in or under

The small woman is best steering away from large patterned garments or vertical prints which overwhelm her small physique. Large accessories like big sunglasses, spectacles, large handbags, chunky jewellery and pendants and big draping scarves or shawls can also overwhelm. Even a big watch face can commandeer the small woman's look.

- The smaller we are, the more petite and lighter the accessories. Glasses, sunglasses, handbags, watches and jewellery are best kept small.
- I recommend the smaller the woman, the narrower the belt she wears.
- Neat and small hats enhance the small woman's look. A big-brimmed hat is over-powering. The pillbox hat or a light fascinator is perfect for the small woman at weddings and race events etc.
- I recommend the smaller the woman, the lower the heel. Small women can be taken over by heels that are too high as

the proportions can look wrong. A petite woman looks best if the heel is narrow and she steers away from clunky platforms or wedges.

- The short woman also looks great wearing monochrome - one colour on top and bottom where possible. It gives the illusion of height if that's what she wants.
- The small woman's look is also enhanced by colour-matching trousers and shoes when possible.
- Steer away from Capris or cropped pants which break the vertical lines of the legs and make them look shorter.
- Dress and skirt hemlines are most flattering at the knee or above. The best hem length for the shorter woman is a few inches above the knee.
- Keep the torso tidy and sleek by tucking in shirts and tops.
- Ankle boots can visually break the vertical line and make the legs look shorter.

Dressing and accessorising proportionately to our small size is especially important in business where we want to

exude authority.

Dressing the Medium to Tall Woman
The Medium-height Woman: 160cm - 170cm/ 5ft 3in - 5ft 7in

THE TALL WOMAN: OVER 170CM/OVER 5FT 7IN

- The taller the woman, the wider the belt she looks best in.
- The taller the person, the longer the heel can be. The six-inch stiletto is ideal for the lightweight, willowy woman. A high but chunky heel looks best on the larger-sized tall woman. Strappy shoes are perfect for the taller woman with longer feet.
- Patterns and prints are bigger too if we want to keep

everything proportional to height. Intricate and small patterns in fabrics can unbalance the taller woman's look.

- The tall woman can wear different blocks of colours on top and bottom to break the long vertical line if she wishes to give the illusion of being shorter.
- Wearing tops *over* bottoms rather than tucked in can look best especially if the waist has no definition.
- Cropped pants also have the effect of shortening the leg.
- Longer-length jackets, often structured, look great on the taller woman rather than a short jacket.

I always think of the late Princess Di when I think of the taller woman. She looked spectacular when she wore longer jackets with a dress underneath because they skimmed over her waistline, which was straight rather than defined.

Hat Tip:

The smaller the woman, the smaller the hat that looks best on her. The taller the woman, the bigger the hat can be. The colour of the hat refers to whatever colour is worn on the shoulder. If wearing a purple dress and a grey coat, the colour of the hat is best kept grey. Add a ribbon or trim in purple to link to the dress, but the primary colour is linked to whatever is worn on the shoulder.

HOW TO DRESS FOR OUR BODY SHAPES

Round, Pear, Inverted Triangle, Rectangle and Hourglass body shapes

To look our absolute best, we can learn which styles best complement our body shape and our lines. Knowing our body type helps us present an attractive and proportional silhouette and helps us flatter all body areas and enhance our best ones. To dress for our body shape is all about following our shape and our bodyline.

As with everything in this book, this is a general guide, not a rulebook. Our bodies are our own and unique to us, so if we love a certain style, we stick with it. Once we're happy and confident in how we look, that's all that matters!

The reason to learn about our body shape is that it gives us great freedom when it comes to dressing, shopping and fashion trends.

Once we learn our shape and how to dress it, our wardrobes become more streamlined and shopping for clothes becomes a much simpler experience.

We can tell right away whether a garment will be flattering for us and can avoid expensive mistakes like buying clothes we never wear!

We also buy what looks best on us rather than what is fashionable or looks good on someone else.

Important Note On Body Shape:

To dress well for our body type, the priority is to wear the correct fabrics and textures for our shape.

RECTANGLE

*H*ow do I know if I have a rectangle-shaped body?

The rectangle shape is the same size top and bottom. Our shoulders, bust and hips are the same width, and there is no defined or 'nipped-in' waist.

The Rectangle Shape:

When asked, many of us reply we are either pear-shaped or hour-glass-shaped. In fact, we are far more likely to be rectangle because this is the most common shape of all in Ireland and the UK. The rectangle describes the woman who is a straight line from her shoulders, waist and hips. She doesn't have much waist definition and her shoulders, bust and hips are the same widths.

The Duchess of Cambridge Kate Middleton is a rectangle shape, and she looks wonderful when she's wearing her country look with a structured tweed jacket, straight jeans and straight knee-high boots. She also looks elegant and regal in structured coats, suits and dresses.

- The rectangle-shaped woman's lines are straight, and her look is enhanced by stiff fabrics and styles that are also straight or structured.

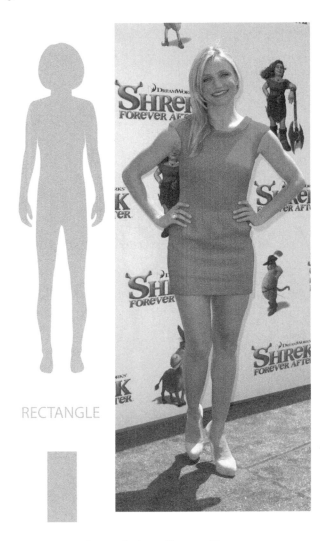

RECTANGLE

Rectangle shape: Cameron Diaz

- She looks her best in structured garments with set-in sleeves. A blazer or smart, structured jacket - slightly fitted if the waistline allows - looks well on the rectangle-shaped woman.

- She looks great in collared linen or cotton shirts, straight trousers, straight dresses like shift dresses and straight skirts or structured A-line or trumpet skirts.
- Wrap dresses with a structured collar can also work well on this body shape, as they nip in and create a waist.
- To create the appearance of a smaller waist, she can go for peplum tops to add volume to the hips.

The Rectangle Shape and Weight:

When this shape woman puts on weight, she puts it on her middle and becomes a typical 'apple' or round shape.

Fabrics:

Structured and stiff fabrics like linen, cotton, denim, tightly woven tweed, boucle, brocade, gaberdine wool, raw silk, taffeta and leather.

Prints:

Plain coloured fabrics or checks or stripes suit best. Try to stay away from polka dots and floral prints – anything with a rounded print. The taller the rectangle-shaped woman is, the bigger the pattern she wears. The smaller her figure is, the smaller the print she looks best in.

Rectangle Woman's Accessories:

Everything angular looks best. Belt buckles are square or rectangular. The face of the watch is more attractive when it's angular rather than round. Angular earrings and pendants look better on the rectangle-shaped woman. Handbags are square or rectangle. Hats that look structured and angular rather than soft and round look amazing. Highlight long and slender arms with sleeveless tops and stacked bracelets. Look for square links in bracelets.

Rectangle celebrities:

Jennifer Aniston, Cameron Diaz, Nicole Kidman, Duchess of Cambridge Kate Middleton

PEAR

*H*ow do I know if I have a pear-shaped body?

The pear-shaped body is larger on the bottom half than on top. Those of us who take a size 16 in pants and skirts and a size 14 on top are pear shapes.

The Pear Shape:

I'm a pear shape myself, and I've always been aware of my bum. So, I always enhance my upper body with patterns, prints, scarves and jewellery, and then I flatter my bottom half by keeping everything soft and simple.

The pear is usually straight on top and curvy on the end, so she's a mix of two body types. That's why I always had trouble wearing suits. The bottom half was always too structured for my body type. As a result, I always wear separates. I wear a stiffer, tailored jacket and very soft, fluid trousers or a fluid skirt underneath.

- Dresses often fail to complement the pear-shaped woman because of the lack of balance between the smaller top and the larger bottom. I often find dresses from LK Bennett seem to find the right balance for pears.

- Skirts are best kept soft, skimming and straight. Think of the pear-shaped royal, Sarah Ferguson. She changed from wide, pleated and patterned skirts to soft fitted skirts and structured jackets, which made her look far more elegant.

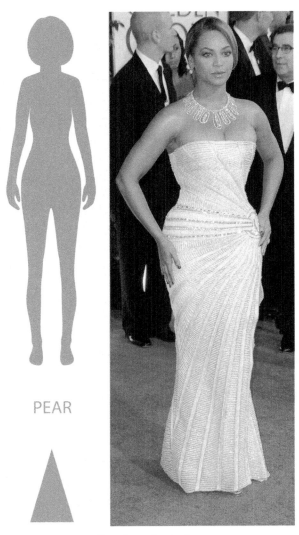

PEAR

Pear shape: Beyoncé

- The pear-shaped woman who wants to balance her proportions with her bottom half is recommended to steer clear of anything sleeveless and to wear V-necks with collars.
- She can broaden the shoulders with details like collars, boat-necks, cowl-necks, puff shoulders, pads, buttons, epaulettes or shawls.
- The bottom half is best when it's kept plain and simple without pockets, buttons or anything that adds bulk or draws the eye.

The Pear Shape and Weight:

When the pear shape gains weight, it accumulates most in the hips, thighs and bum area.

Fabrics:

On top, the pear-shaped woman can wear structured, stiff fabrics such as linen, cotton, denim, tightly woven tweed, boucle, brocade, gaberdine wool, raw silk, taffeta and leather.

On the bottom, she is best wearing loosely woven, soft and draping fabrics like jersey, chiffon, light crepe wool, silk satin, cashmere and lambs wool, lycra, polyester, velour, voile and lace.

Prints:

Keep it dark, monochrome or neutral colours on the bottom half and save any brightly coloured prints for the top only. The taller the pear-shaped woman is, the bigger the pattern she can wear, and the smaller her figure, the smaller the print can be.

.   .   .

Pear Women's Accessories:

Jewellery looks best when it is circular or oval-shaped. The bag can be straight on top if it is oval on the bottom. The rounded satchel shape is ideal or an oval baguette bag. The pear woman can wear both rounded and pointy shoes. If the foot is broad, go for a pointed shoe. If the foot is narrower, the square or rounded toe looks good.

Pear Celebrities:

Kim Kardashian West, Beyoncé, Rihanna, Duchess of York Sarah Ferguson, Princess Beatrice.

ROUND

*H*ow do I know if I have a round-shaped body?

The round-shaped body has a similar circumference at the shoulders, bust, waist but are often widest in the middle. Those of us who have trouble with gaping lower shirt buttons and tight waistbands are often a round shape.

The Round Shape:

Women who have an upper body that may be bigger than the lower body with a wide midriff are referred to as round-shaped or apple-shaped.

Some women are just born round, and some women, who have put on weight in their middles, become round-shaped.

At times in my life, I've put on weight and I've become a round shape rather than pear-shaped. When I was taking antidepressants, hormonal treatment and the fertility drug, Clomid, I certainly gained weight.

I have been a size 18 in the past, but people wouldn't have known because I dressed it well.

There are several things can do for this body type to create more of a visual balance and create more of an illusion of the coveted hourglass figure.

- I know from experience that if I wore bulkier fabrics and structured garments, I looked heavier.
- Once I kept my fabrics soft and fluid and plain, it was easier to disguise the weight gain.
- Keep the necklines low - a V-neckline has an elongating effect. A scooped neck is also flattering, but a crew neck or any detail around the neck adds bulk to the mid-section. Square and boat necklines can also have a widening effect.
- Stick to soft flowing A-line or tunic styles in draping fabrics which can be more complementary than figure-hugging tops or T-shirts.
- The empire line dress is a good choice for the round woman as it cinches the narrowest part of our body, which is under the bust. The swing dress or trapeze dress is also great, especially for younger round woman.
- Trousers look best on the round shape when they are straight cut.
- Depending on our legs, we can wear hemlines long or short.
- Keep sleeves soft and full length or three-quarter length.

ROUNDED

Round shape: Melissa McCarthy

Jackets are best at hip level and not cropped. Flared coats for winter look great.

- Fitted or structured garments are not enhancing as they make the round woman look square.

- The structured appearance of anything with pleats is not a great look for the round body shape.

The Round Shape and Weight:

When this shape figure puts on weight, it is distributed all over rather than in specific areas.

Fabrics:

The round woman looks best in soft, fluid and draping fabrics like jersey, chiffon, light crepe wool, silk satin, cashmere and lambs' wool, lycra, polyester, velour, voile and lace.

Prints:

The round woman's look is enhanced by keeping it plain and simple. Monochrome colours look best. Patterns and prints are not usually recommended for the round woman to look her best.

Round Women's Accessories:

Look great by wearing less clutter! A single piece of jewellery rather than layered beads and bangles looks best. A single dramatic neck-lace or pendant in the V-neckline looks terrific. Try long, narrow earrings that elongate the face, and bring attention to the upper body. Belts may serve to highlight a lack of definition around the waist. The round woman's shoes are best kept to a soft round toe rather than a point. Keep bags softly rounded but not bulky.

Round Celebrities:

Oprah Winfrey is an hourglass body type who becomes a round shape when she puts on weight. Dawn French, Melissa McCarthy,

Rebel Wilson, Queen Latifah, Adele, Beth Ditto, Kelly Clarkson and Kelly Osbourne have all been round body types at some stages in their lives.

INVERTED TRIANGLE

*H*ow do I know if I'm an inverted triangle?

Inverted triangles are usually a larger size on top and a smaller size on the bottom. Wearing a size 14 on top, for example, and a size 12 in pants or skirts, indicates an inverted triangle shape.

The Inverted Triangle Shape:

This shape, with its broad shoulders, is the most athletic looking body type, and the silhouette is also common among top models. The inverted triangle is characterised by broad shoulders, a small waistline and slim hips.

My recommendation is to balance the top half of the body with the smaller bottom half.

- Wearing V-necklines gives the illusion of narrowing the shoulders.
- Tops with V-necks and collars look good, and the halter neck was invented for the younger inverted triangle-shaped woman. Women of a certain age look better with sleeves

once the elasticity has gone in the upper arms. The movement or the wobble of the arms draws the eye away from better parts of our look.

- The set-in sleeve is the best look for the inverted triangle shape because the raglan sleeve is going to make the shoulders look broader.
- The boatneck collar has a widening effect on the inverted triangle shaped body.
- This shape looks best when it's dressed in upper garments which are structured rather than floaty. Single-breasted fitted jackets, crisp shirts, straight trousers, wide trousers, straight shift dresses, straight or structured A-line skirts add excellent balance to the inverted triangle shape.
- Cropped tops, high collars and short jackets are not usually flattering to the inverted triangle shape. The look can become top heavy rather than balanced.
- Floaty or swing tops are not usually flattering to this shape either.
- Try darker, neutral colours on top. Give the illusion of balance by wearing brighter colours on the bottom half.

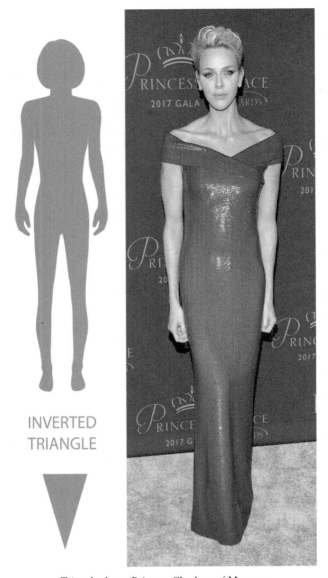

Triangle shape: Princess Charlene of Monaco

The Inverted Triangle and Weight:

The inverted triangle tends to put weight on her upper body usually the shoulders and bustline, but the waist can thicken too.

· · ·

Fabrics:

Structured, stiff fabrics like linen, cotton, denim, tightly woven tweed, boucle, brocade, gaberdine wool, raw silk, taffeta and leather.

Prints:

Steer away from prints, patterns and details on top. Also, go for stripes and checks rather than floral prints or dots on the bottom half. The taller the inverted triangle woman is, the bigger the pattern she can wear, and the smaller her size, the smaller the print can be.

Inverted Triangle Accessories:

Try to keep bags angular and at hip level. Look for an alternative to chunky necklaces as they add clutter and bulk to the top half. Instead, look for long pendants or big chunky bracelets and bangles which draw the eyes to slim hips. Hats are best structured, with wide flat brims.

Inverted Triangle celebrities:

Duchess of Sussex Megan Markle, Princess Charlene of Monaco, Naomi Campbell, Demi Moore, Renee Zellweger, Cindy Crawford, Charlize Theron.

HOURGLASS

*H*ow do I know if I have an hourglass-shaped body?

Hourglass-shaped bodies are the same size on the bust and the hips and have a very defined waist. Those of us who wear the same size in trousers and tops and have a smaller waist are hourglass-shaped.

The Hourglass Shape

The curvier hourglass-shaped body is exemplified by voluptuous Hollywood icons like Marilyn Monroe, Sofia Loren, Jayne Mansfield and Raquel Welsh. The hourglass is a shape that is much admired and is the easiest to identify. Hourglass shapes are characterised by a proportionate top and bottom part of the body with a curvy 'nipped-in' waistline. Hourglass bodies are regarded as very feminine and balanced.

This body type is naturally balanced and is relatively easy to dress once garments are soft, draping and hugging the curves. It's all about soft fabrics for the hourglass-shaped woman. Designer Jean

Louis knew just how to flatter Marilyn's hourglass shape when he created the figure-hugging, fluid gown she wore as she sang Happy Birthday Mr President to John F Kennedy.

- Anything fluid, body-skimming and form-fitting that hugs and accentuates the hourglass figure's curves look best.

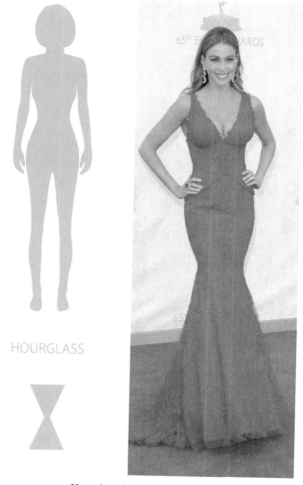

HOURGLASS

Hourglass shape: Sofia Vergara

- Structured jackets and leather or denim jackets tend to make the hourglass shape look 'boxy'. Think of Dolly Parton or Marilyn Monroe in denim jackets. Their gorgeous curves would be concealed under the bulkiness of the fabric.

- Dresses, tops, trousers and skirts that are fitted and flowing are flattering for the hourglass figure.
- V-necks are wonderful on those with a great cleavage.

The hourglass and weight:

The hourglass shape becomes a round shape when she puts on weight because she usually loses her defined waistline.

Hourglass Accessories:

Look for alternatives to sharp, angular shapes. Belts with rounded or oval buckles accentuate the hourglass figure. Handbags look best with curved edges. The hourglass figure's jewellery is best round and oval rather than angular. The best watch is oval or round, and even bracelet links are rounded. The hourglass shape will look best in hats which have soft curves too. A rounded toe on the shoe works well unless the foot is wide when a pointed toe is always recommended.

Fabrics:

Loosely woven, soft and draping fabrics like jersey, chiffon, light crepe wool, silk satin, cashmere and, lycra, polyester, velour, voile and lace.

Prints:

Steer away from checks and stripes as they don't enhance the curved shape of the hourglass. They can wear soft polka dot, floral or abstract prints, especially with curves. The taller the hourglass woman is, the bigger the pattern she can wear, and the smaller her size, the smaller the print can be. If in doubt, forget printed fabrics, and keep fabrics plain and monochrome.

Hourglass-shape Celebrities:

Sofia Vergara, Salma Hayek, Dita Von Teese, Christina Hendrick, Jennifer Lopez.

HOW TO FLATTER OUR BODY AREAS

*I*t's how we feel about ourselves that matters, so the following simple suggestions only apply if there is some part of your body that you would like to enhance or flatter over another.

It's easy to flatter our body in the online world where there are photo apps and reshaping tools that let us resize our waists, our breasts, our legs and reinvent ourselves.

However, with a few clever optical illusions and simple tricks, it's not too difficult to complement our appearances in real-life too.

We can visually change our body shapes by being clever with shapes, patterns, styles and even colour.

The number one tip for dressing to highlight our best assets and draw all the attention there.

I'm a pear shape so I use the oldest trick in the book to draw attention away from my bum by highlighting my face and hair with bright colours on top, great earrings and neck pieces and the right shades of lipstick!

Here are a few tricks and tips that I've learnt down the years which flatter body areas and make the most of our best bits so we go out brimming with confidence, and looking fabulous!

THE NECK

Short Necks

Necklines are very important. We can change our looks entirely and look leaner or taller by just changing our neck lines.

- Women with shorter necks look best wearing a V-neck, open neck shirts, or scooped necklines.
- A V-neck sweater or top elongates the neck while a crew neck shortens it.
- For those with more angular faces, boat-necks and scooped necklines are often more flattering than V-necks.
- Anyone with a short neck looks best without wearing higher necklines, scarves tied around the neck, chokers or short necklaces.
- Jewellery and scarves is best worn long and low to bring the eye down and give the illusion of length.

Wide Necks

- Anyone with a wide neck and broad shoulders, which is common with those who have put on weight, look best when they expose the neck and don't clutter the area with jewellery.
- They are enhanced by the lengthening look of the V-neck.
- Collars with V-necks are good too as the collar gives height and narrows the shoulders and the V-neckline takes the eye down low.
- A soft, draping cowl-neck also works if it exposes the neckline.
- Jewellery and scarves are best be worn long and low to bring the eye down and give an illusion of greater slenderness.
- The right hair can also work wonders. A sharp bob at chin level will widen the face and make the neck look more elegant by comparison. Hair worn below the shoulder will also soften the wider neck.

Thin Neck

- Open or plunging necklines are not flattering if we have lost a lot of weight or have a naturally thin neck.
- Build up the neckline with collared shirts under jackets and jumpers for example – anything that gives a layering effect.
- If we have a long thin neck, we can wear Mandarin collars, polo necks or wear colourful silk or light wool scarves over crew necks

Long Necks

- A long neck or 'swan neck' is elegant and the look is enhanced by polo necks, turtlenecks, Mandarin and Nehru collars and stand-up collars.
- Women with long necks can also call wear simple crew necks with aplomb and choose to add width by wearing a slash or boat neckline.
- Those with long necks look wonderful with scarves, chunky chokers and rows of beads worn wrapped around the neck or close to the base of the neck.

THE SHOULDERS

$\mathcal{N}$arrow Shoulders

The only way we have shoulders that appear to be too narrow is to have wider hips. Those who believe they have narrow shoulders are probably a classic pear shape. If we're a size 12 on top and a size 14 on the bottom, then we can to balance the two halves of our body by making our shoulders look wider.

- V-neck tops make narrow shoulders look even narrower.
- Try boat necks or slash necks to create a horizontal line that widens the look at the shoulders.
- Look for shirts with a double lapel to give the illusion of width.

- Look for puff sleeves, padded shoulders or sleeves with details or epaulettes at the shoulders.
- Try scarves, wraps, fur collars, shawls and shrugs or just hang a jumper over the shoulders. These accessories help to create a balance between narrow shoulders and wider hips.
- Jackets with structured shoulders are also a good friend to the woman with narrow shoulders!

Broad Shoulders

Most models have good, broad shoulders, which makes them excellent clothes horses. We also often talk about athletic women, especially swimmers, when we refer to broad-shouldered women. For those who wish to flatter this area, here are a few suggestions.

- The V-neck and vertical detail such as buttons are the friends of women who want to complement broad shoulders and balance them with the bottom half of the body.
- Keep tops and jackets simple and structured with V-necks and sharp lapels if possible.
- For balance, steer away from any details on the shoulders including puff sleeves or shoulder pads.
- Wear scarves draped down the body not across the shoulders or around the neck.
- Necklaces and pendants look best when they are also draped long and down the body.

THE BUST

The Large Bust

Buxom women are curvy and feminine and to enhance their look, I recommend that keeping the upper half streamlined and simple.

- Steer clear of pockets or pleats, frills, fur collars and anything that adds chunkiness around the bust area.
- The best necklines for the woman with a large bust are V-shaped. A V-cleavage brings balance with the lower half of the body because it gives the illusion of a smaller bust and a longer torso.
- Jewellery that collects or 'pools' on the bust will add bulk to the area.
- Be aware that half-sleeves or sleeves that end at our elbows have a widening effect at bust level.

- Keep fabrics plain, simple and soft. Stiff fabrics look 'boxy' on the large breasted woman.
- Bright, shiny fabrics will also enhance the bust size while darker, matte fabrics will make the bust recede.

The Small Bust

The beauty about having a small bust is that the options for tops are limitless. The small breasted woman looks good in prints, flounces, sequins and lace.

- For those who wish to make more with less, begin with the bra. Push-up and padded bras help when we want to make a small bust look bigger.
- Look for tops with pockets, pleats, buttons and bulkier, structured fabrics for added balance if the bottom half is bigger than the top half.
- Off-the-shoulder tops or backless tops are great for the small bustline as they redirect the eyes to erogenous zones like the shoulders and back.
- A waist-cinching belt also draws the eye to a trim waist rather than the chest area.
- Plunging V-necklines are not always flattering. Look for boat and slash necklines instead.
- Fur collars, scarves, wraps and piles of big jewellery add more visual volume to the upper half of the body too.

THE WAISTLINE

*L*ong Waists

I'm a medium height woman, and I always get on my toes when I try on trousers. That's a sure sign that I'm trying to lengthen my legs and that I'm a long-waisted woman.

Having a long waist means that our legs are short in proportion to the torso. If we wish to achieve a balanced look, we give the illusion of shortening the body line and lengthening the legs.

- The most flattering length for tops on the long-waisted woman is crotch level and above. Any hem that falls below this line will have the illusion of lengthening the waist further.
- Cropped tops, boleros, short tops all work well. The Chanel-style jacket is ideal for those with long waists.
- Tuck tops and shirts inside the waistband.
- If the waistline is trim, wear belts. When wearing dresses, make sure to have detail at the waist especially for special occasions like a wedding dress.
- Turn-ups on trousers and cropped pants create the illusion of shortening the length of legs.

Short Waists

Having a short waist means our legs are long in proportion to our torso. The typical body shape is someone with a bigger bust and long legs and a waist that is not very defined. If we want to bring balance and enhance this body shape, we can make the body line or torso look longer.

- The best length for tops on the short-waisted woman is crotch level and below. Any hem that falls above this line will have the illusion of shortening the waist further and making the top half of the body look bulky.
- The Chanel-style jacket looks boxy on the short waisted woman, but the longer jacket is perfect for those with short waists.

- The V-neck has a lengthening effect on the torso.
- Balance the torso and legs with turn-ups on the trousers.
- Skim over the waistline area if it is not defined. I suggest that we do not tuck tops into the waistband and we stay away from belts unless they are falling into a 'V'.
- Short waisted women suit shift dresses, flowing empire-line dresses and trapeze dresses rather than dresses that are cinched at the waist.

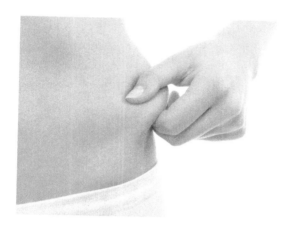

Wide Waists

The wide waisted woman is often an apple shape or someone who tends to put on weight around her middle. Women with this body type often have big shoulders, a large bust line, a soft middle and narrower hips.

- For an instant tightening effect, we can lose the lumps and bumps with body sculpting shapewear and control underwear like Spanx. Modern foundation garments are a great option for a streamline effect when we need to look our best!
- The rest of the time, soft flowing A-line or tunic styles in draping fabrics are more complementary to wide waists than figure-hugging tops or T-shirts

- A V-neckline also lengthens the torso and draws attention from the wide waist especially if the wide-waisted woman has a good cleavage!
- The shift dress will fit and flatter the apple shape and skim over the middle area. The empire line dress is also a good choice as it cinches the narrowest part of the body shape, which is under the bust. The swing dress or trapeze dress is great especially for younger wide-waisted woman.
- Of course, focusing all the attention on another body part ensures a wide waist will fade into the background. Concentrate on the face and neck, for example, by adding vibrant jewellery and lip colour or display those perfect pins with a short shift or trapeze dress and nosebleed high heels!

Note On Jacket Length:

The perfect length blazer or jacket for everyone is the one that ends just at the crotch level or just above the wrist and just where the bum ends. The point where our wrist ends is usually about the halfway point on our body.

THE ARMS

Long Arms

When our sleeves always look too short, and we're always tugging at our sleeve ends, we know we have long arms!

Long arms look great with chunky bracelets, a big watch and turned-up sleeves, half sleeves and sleeves with large cuffs.

Short Arms

If sleeves always dangle well past our wrist and we're always rolling them up or turning up the hem, we know we have short arms.

Those with shorter arms look great in three-quarter length sleeves or rolled-up sleeves. Chunkier jewellery makes the arm look shorter and bulkier.

.   .   .

Upper Arms

When we gain weight, fat tends to settle in our upper arm and as we age, the skin and muscle tone softens. So here are my suggestions to flatter upper arms.

- String tops, thin straps and halter-necks will make upper arms look bigger.
- Tops with wider shoulder straps and a V-neckline will make arms look more toned.
- Short sleeves which cover the top and the widest part of the upper arm are great for summer while batwing sleeves, raglan sleeves and full sleeves are ideal at other times of the year.
- Beware of cap sleeves which end at the widest part of the arm because that is where the eye will fall.
- Wraps, boleros, shawls and scarves are also a great addition to a sleeveless or short sleeved outfit if we're feeling a bit 'exposed' in the arm area.

WIDE OR NARROW FINGERS

Dainty rings with small stones are not flattering as they will accentuate the size of the fingers. We can lengthen our digits by wearing a ring that runs the length of our fingers in a long oval, diamond or rectangle shape. If we have very thin fingers, we are best to go for a wide band-shaped ring that gives the illusion of width.

THE LEGS AND HIPS

 Wide Hips

- Curvy hips, thighs and bum are complemented with fluid fabrics that skim the body. Stiff or bulky fabrics like denim look 'boxy' and wide on our curves.
- It's best to steer clear of pockets, flounces or other details that add bulk and keep the look darker, plain and simple.
- We can enhance our bottom half with wider leg pants or boot cut pants rather than straight or skinny pants. The look is best when it is fitted but not skin-tight.
- Low-waist or low-slung pants are not flattering as they enhance width.

- The long, fluid wrap dress is perfect for those with wide hips or thighs.
- Add all the colour, details and eye-catching accessories to the top half of the body to keep the eye's attention there.
- Adding a pair of high heels when we can, adds length and slenderness to the bottom half.

Short Legs

- The woman with short legs is best suited to dress and skirt hemlines that are knee-length or above.
- We look best wearing short jackets and tops that end at the waist if we have short legs.
- Cropped pants or those with turn-ups make the legs look wider and shorter. Baggy pants have the same effect.
- Straight leg pants suit the shorter leg by making them appear longer.
- Adding shoes with pointy toes and heels especially in a matching colour with pants makes the leg look even longer.
- Women with short legs and a long waist look great in high-waisted pants. They shorten the look of the torso and also give the illusion of lengthening the legs.

Long Legs

- The woman with longer legs is best suited to dress and skirt hemlines that are knee-length or below.
- Wide-leg pants like flowing palazzos often help balance the leggy lady with her torso.
- Capri pants, cropped trousers and those with turn-ups can also help to attain a more balanced look.

Heavy Calves or Thick Ankles

Victorian men swooned at the sight of a well-turned ankle in the days when skirts swept to the floor. These days, they have far more to focus on than a less than perfect ankle.

When women naturally retain weight or fluid in their lower legs and ankles, there is little that they can do about them except make them less noticeable.

Here are a few dressing tips for lower legs that don't involve wearing riding boots or ankle boots year-round!

- Flat shoes can emphasise big calves and ankles so, where possible, go with the lengthening look of a heel, even a medium heel height.
- A chunkier shoe heel balances out a heavy looking lower leg or ankle, so wedges or platform heels are perfect for this leg ending.
- A pointy toe or a soft round toe and a low shoe vamp also lengthen the foot and make it look lighter.
- Shoes with a matte finish like suede are also more forgiving than shiny patent finishes for the heavier lower leg.
- Match the colour of the shoe to the tights. For example, match nude shoes to skin-coloured tights for an even longer look.
- Strappy slave sandals, skinny stilettos and delicate or fussy shoes are not flattering. They draw attention to the area and give the illusion of larger ankles or calves.
- A pencil thin skirt accentuates the wider leg, so stick to the wider A-line cut skirt to give more balance to the wider leg.
- Wearing a hem that hovers below the widest part of the calf also gives the illusion of a narrower leg. A hemline that ends at midcalf emphasises the widest part of the leg.
- When the rest of the world seems to be wearing hot pants

and shorts, a pair of flowing palazzo pants can make women with heavy calves look cool and stylish. Bootcut or fluid wide pants are a great friend to those of us with heavy legs.
- Divert all the attention to the top half of the body with brighter colours fabrics and accessories.

Wide Foot

Anyone with a broad foot can flatter it with a deep vamp in the shoe and a pointed toe to give the illusion of a narrower look.

Long Foot

Steer away from shoes that have a low vamp as they elongate the look further. Shoes with a higher vamp or with straps, buckles and details look amazing and give the illusion of a shorter foot. Aim for an oval, round or square toe rather than a pointed one.

Small Foot

Straps and details make the small foot look chunky. Those with petite feet can flatter them with simplicity of style, an elegantly pointed toe and a longer vamp in the shoe.

THE WARDROBE MAKEOVER

J'm a big fan of the capsule wardrobe because it leads to effortless style! I saw the capsule wardrobe in action for the first time when I went to Canada. My friend Jean went to work every morning looking professional and smart in a different look every day. It seemed like she had dozens of outfits but when she showed me her wardrobe, all she had were twelve items in neutral and complementary shades.

The idea of a capsule wardrobe is to build a compact collection of clothes, a bare minimum of pieces, that all perfectly mix and match with each other with ease.

Before I was trained, I had a wardrobe that was packed to capacity with beautiful clothes, and still I felt like I had nothing to wear.

Now I know that the minimalist, perfectly pared down wardrobe contains only top-quality, long-lasting pieces in great fabrics and in complementary colours. It means that getting dressed in the morning is a process that is simple, speedy and easy.

I recommend that capsule wardrobe is filled with items suitable for the life we have, rather than the fantasy life we never live or an old life that we no longer live! If we have clothes in our wardrobe that are two sizes too small and we haven't worn them in years, it may be time to move them to a better home!

If we have sequinned tops and satin pants and haven't been on a dance floor in a decade, they may be more useful to someone else too.

When buying clothes, my suggestion is to spend most of our money on the clothes we spend most of the time wearing.

If we spend eight or more hours a day and five days a week in the office, then most of our spending is best aimed at business wear. If we are stay-at-home mums, retired women or we work from home, we are best concentrating our spending on a more casual wardrobe.

There is no limit to the size of the capsule wardrobe. For some, it's thirty pieces and for others it may be hundreds of garments. However, the whole idea of the capsule wardrobe is to spend less time and money on shopping and less time on dressing.

Twelve essential pieces is the minimum for a good capsule wardrobe. Try to buy neutral and complementary shades, beige, navy or grey separates and cream or soft white tops for example. The don't have to be the same shade or beige, navy or grey to be mixed and matched.

Just remember, everyone's capsule wardrobe is going to look different because we all have our own unique style, different bodies, distinct colouring, changing lifestyles and diverging tastes.

The following capsule collection offers a few basic suggestions that can be tailored to suit our individual bodies and lifestyles.

NEUTRAL MINIMALISTIC COLOR PALETTE

WHITE	IVORY	CREAM	LIGHT GREY
BABY BLUE	SAND	NUDE	BEIGE
CAMEL	CARAMEL	TAN	TAUPE
MARINE	GREY	KHAKI	OLIVE
NAVY	BROWN	CHARCOAL	BLACK

12 CAPSULE WARDROBE BASICS

*F*or the capsule wardrobe to work, we select each piece to suit our colour palette and our body size and shape. I always recommend choosing classic and timeless garments and versatile pieces that are easy to mix and match so that we can extend their use and get real value for money.

7 Tops

2 shirts:

A quality silk shirt for the office will also work for night when dressed up with pearls or a glamorous choker.

A crisp white or off-white button-down shirt is great both for the office and for casual wear. Cotton and linen shirts are not suitable for round and hourglass body shapes, who are better opting for two silk blouses.

Alternatively, they can opt for a soft button-up top or change the ratios of the other tops below.

2 camisoles or T-shirts:

A silk camisole which is either strappy, scoop neck or crew neck works under a blazer or a cardigan in the office environment and can also be dressed up at night. For the more casual working and living environment, two quality, plain T-shirts in a light and dark colour will also work.

1 long sleeve tee:

A good quality soft and long sleeve tee will add lots more versatility to the working and the casual wardrobe.

1 sweater:

A lightweight and soft sweater in good quality cashmere, for example, will suit most body types. Bulkier sweaters can be worn by rectangles and pear-shapes. The sweater will be more useful if it's a shade that can be worn over all three bottoms listed below.

1 cardigan:

The cardigan adds versatility in a changeable climate. It offers a softer look to a structured blazer. Depending on body shape, it can be long or short and in a shade that can be worn over all the other tops listed and all three bottoms listed below.

3 Bottoms

2 pairs of trousers:

One dress pair of wool trousers for the office or for evening wear and one casual like denims or chinos is ideal. Two pairs of casual trousers are more suitable for those of us who have a more casual lifestyle. Medium-wash jeans are best because they can work with everything in our closet.

1 skirt:

The skirt is best in a similar shade to the trousers. Obviously, the person who prefers skirts, just changes the ratio between trousers and skirts.

1 good dress:

One timeless and classic sheath or wrap dress in navy, for example, is ideal as it can be worn to the office and dressed up for evening wear. Most people think of the LBC (little black dress) as their go-to dress, but I've expressed my feelings about black at this stage! Find a dress in a good neutral colour and a shape that flatters.

1 good jacket:

This can be a fitted blazer for the office or a more casual jacket for the non-office going woman. Ensure that you buy a neutral colour that will work with everything else in the wardrobe.

The Rest of Our Wardrobe

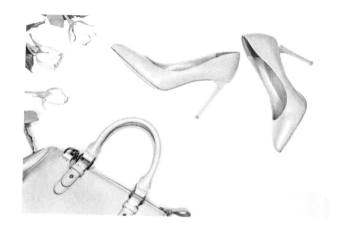

Shoes:

A flat pair of shoes, a pair of casual shoes like runners and one pair of classic court shoes are all that is required for a good capsule wardrobe. Of course, I would have a lot more money if I followed my own recommendations!

I always advocate spending money on good quality leather shoes. In a mad moment when I was making money and feeling flush, I bought a pair of designer Christian Louboutin shoes. Even so, I remember gasping at the price tag.

But that must have been about twelve years ago, and those black stiletto shoes are still gorgeous. They are worn a lot because I love them, and I am very hard on shoes. Yet even after all these years, they look absolutely perfect; they're like the day I bought them.

Sometimes it's worth spending more, because the more we spend on shoes, the longer they will last.

The Winter Coat:

For women who drive everywhere or whose lifestyle is casual, the traditional winter coat is optional. An extra-warm jacket will suffice.

However, if commuting to and from the office involves walking, a good, classic wool coat is a smart investment that can last decades.

Handbags:

There's nothing like a really good handbag and shoes to elevate a gal's confidence and her look. I always recommend that we invest in one or two exceptionally good handbags in neutral colours like black, beige or navy and in a classic design.

Investment purchases are the way to go for businesswomen. I have a Chanel bag which was an expensive purchase, but I'm wearing it for years, and I plan to wear it for decades more. I also have a little Louis Vuitton bag which I've worn for years too. I even have a Hermes Birkin bag, which I bought as a present for myself for a very special birthday.

All three are made with quality materials, so they are always going to look smart and elegant. If I look after them, they will even be an investment and won't lose their value. I really believe in buying the best that we can afford. And even if we can't afford it right now, we can save up for it in the future. We all deserve something elegant and timeless!

Gloves:

Look for a pair of good quality Italian leather gloves that will last for years and look better as they age.

Accessories:

Pashminas, shrugs, wraps and scarves can change our look in an instant. Stick to good quality cashmere, wool, silk and satin items that will look great year after year.

Underwear:

The right fitting bras are essential for a good silhouette so it's worth getting properly fitted and to buy good quality support.

I'm a great advocate of Spanx for a great streamlined silhouette especially for evening wear. Look out for the Spanx Oncore Open Bust Bodysuit, which sits just under the bust. It's lightweight and powerful and has great sculpting effect.

Hosiery:

This is the only thing I am adamant about: tights or nylons are an absolute must for the stylish woman! Whether it is a wedding, funeral, going to the office, attending a business meeting, nylons are vital to a groomed and professional look.

Nylons add finish and polish whenever we wear skirts or dresses. Wear them even in peep-toes shoes and strappy sandals. No, false tan is not enough! Yes, tights are best even in the height of summer.

Andrea Bucci in a natural shade called Caresse are wonderful sheer, shaping tights available in many outlets. The Blush shade in Wolford tights is also particularly good. Pretty Polly is also a recommended brand in hosiery. Satin finish opaque tights are great for winter.

Note on Fabrics with Prints

When buying anything with patterns and prints, aim for 'disposable' fashion pieces. Try not to pay a lot of money for anything with an obvious pattern or print.

For me, prints are noticeable and I retain them in my mind. After a few times wearing the garment, I feel as if I'm wearing the same thing all the time.

I always recommend buying investment pieces in classic and neutral colours like navy, grey or beige. They are colours that are gentle on the eye and can be worn for years!

SUGGESTED FASHION BRANDS

or Casual Wear:

Try brands like Tommy Hilfiger or Ralph Lauren. These are brands that produce smart-casual ranges in classic shapes and colours that we can wear for years. I find I can't wear them out.

Creatives looking for a modern more expressive look can check out the Sarah Pacini collection. Fabrics are soft so are suited to those who are uncomfortable with their weight.

Cos is also simple and affordable for casual wear with good fabrics at a mid-price.

For Business Wear:

When it comes to suits or separates, the Italian labels such as Armani or Max Mara or the German label, Escada, stand out from the crowd. However, they are expensive, so they are investment purchases. They are made from quality fabrics, and if we choose a classic design and a neutral colour, they can be worn forever.

Irish designer Louise Kennedy also produces a range of investment purchases and some separates that are very flattering for body types who can't wear suits. Her garments are magnificent too and made from quality fabrics, in classic designs that last forever.

Brands like Chanel and DKNY are great for the smaller-sized woman who are a neat size 8 or 10.

In the medium price bracket, brands like Phase Eight and Basler produce well-made suits, separates and occasion wear that will last many seasons too.

Note for the Budget Conscious:

Keep an eye on the sales to buy expensive clothes at much reduced prices. Also, regularly check on the stock in good second-hand designer exchange stores. There are incredible bargains to be found in fashion and accessories in 'pre-loved' stores that specialise in designer labels.

Note on Sizes:

Fashion sizes are only a number. They are meant to be a guideline and are not definitive. If you are size 14 and try on an Escada jacket, it will probably fit perfectly because German sizes are comparable to Irish and UK sizes. If you try on an Italian size 14, it will quite likely be too small. It's never advisable to stick to your 'size' and buy anything too small. There is nothing less stylish than clothes that are too tight and gaping.

THE MOTHER OF THE BRIDE AND GROOM MAKEOVER

The big Irish wedding is a great and time-honoured institution in this country.

As a result, many of my image and style clients were first-time mothers of the bride and groom who were anxious about the big day.

Yes, MOBs and MOGs have wedding day jitters too!

As well as analysing the mother of the bride and groom's colours and body styles and discussing the ideal outfit for their shape and size, I often suggest the following simple tips for the matriarchs of the family:

The Colours:

A wedding is over in a day or maybe two, but the wedding photos last forever. What I usually suggest to clients is that they aim to look good for posterity in the wedding photos!

I always advise the mother of the bride to co-ordinate her look with her daughter's bridesmaids. So, if the bridesmaids are wearing baby pink, for example, and the mother of the bride's colour palette is spring, she could look for a coral pink.

If the mother of the bride's palette is winter, she could choose a cerise pink. This palette of pinks will look striking in a photograph.

The mother of the bride can find her own colour palette's version of whatever colour the bridesmaids are wearing whether it's blue, green or lilac.

Then her look will complement the bridesmaids and presumably, the bride's bouquet and that harmonious family look will hang on the wall for the rest of her days.

Ideally, the mother of the groom appears in a different colour from the mother of the bride. She is best taking her cue from the bride and groom.

If the bride is wearing white and the groom is wearing silver or grey, then the mother of the groom can look for something with grey and white. If the groom is wearing navy, she could choose to wear navy and white. She will be standing by the groom in the wedding photos, so will be a very stylish look for the wedding album!

The Jacket:

The mother of the bride or groom buttons or ties her jacket when standing or walking and only unbuttons it when sitting.

The Hat:

Yes, I know I'm repeating myself here, but I can't emphasise it enough – the smaller the woman the smaller her hat can be. The scale is important.

How many times have we seen a small woman at a wedding wearing a big hat? All anybody sees is the big hat. The beautiful mother of the bride or groom is lost somewhere under it, so it appears that the hat is wearing her.

A pill box or a fascinator is ideal for the smaller mother of the bride or groom. However, the same pill box will be lost on a taller or bigger woman. Again, we're talking about scale.

We can also examine our face and body shape (see earlier chapters) to work out which hat will enhance our overall look.

Once again, I'd like to remind everyone that the hat colour is linked to whatever we wear on the shoulder. If the mother of the bride is wearing a baby blue dress and a navy coat, then it is appropriate that her hat is navy. She can wear a baby blue trim on the hat to link to the dress, but the hat is best matching the coat.

Accessories:

I love gloves for a wedding especially if wearing three-quarter length or short sleeves. They look very flattering and elegant at a formal event. I recommend that the gloves match the handbag, and shoes. All three look best in the same colour as the outfit or darker, not lighter. The only exception is for nude colours. If the mother of the groom, for example, is wearing a black and beige outfit, she can accessorise her bag, gloves and shoes in nude or in black.

Hosiery:

No bare legs for the mother of the bride or groom. No, not even in the height of summer!

Why spend a fortune on a wonderful dress or suit, have our hair coiffed and nails polished and then leave the legs in the wild?

Bare legs lack polish and finish, and yet I am constantly surprised by how often I see it.

Just as we wear make-up on our face, I *ALWAYS* recommend wearing tights on exposed legs except when we're on the beach or by the pool.

It's really not optional for a wedding - tights are part of the uniform for occasion and dress wear.

Footwear:

A classic, elegant and shapely court shoe is recommended and always looks best at a wedding.

I prefer not to see the mother of the bride's toes, so I don't recommend open-toed shoes, strappy sandals or peep-toe shoes. Sandals are for evening wear or for running around the beach.

The shoes give an elongated and elegant look when they match or are a shade deeper than the outfit.

MARION'S MANNERS MAKEOVER

Hold the cup and saucer when standing

*D*ining etiquette and table manners are always something I've always believed to be essential as part of my style and image consultations.

Admittedly, I have a bit of an obsession with table manners since I was socially embarrassed at a dinner table as a young girl. It happened soon after my family moved house, and I went from a country school Upper Glanmire National School and then Saint

Vincent's Primary School to a private secondary school in the city called Miss O'Sullivan's Secondary School.

Miss O's, as it was called, was a very different environment to the schools I was used to. I'll always be grateful to the place because I met my two lifelong friends, Jane and Mary, on my first day there.

Before this, I had only ever eaten at home where informality was to be expected. My mother was a wonderful cook and homemaker, but there was no emphasis on dining etiquette in our house. I never heard of such a thing.

Then I was invited to a new schoolfriend's home, where mealtimes were a more formal affair, and one of the girls mocked me and laughed at how I was eating. I felt out of my depth, and I'll never forget the hurt and the fear of that.

'What am I doing wrong?' I asked, the food nearly sticking in my throat with fright.

'Why can't you hold your knife and fork properly?' she laughed.

I still didn't know what I was doing wrong or what she meant. My cheeks burnt with humiliation that day.

Everyone else at that table probably forgot about that incident straightaway, but I couldn't. The first chance I got, I ran to the library and took out books on manners and table etiquette.

I read every page and finally understood that I was holding my knife and fork like they were pens instead of holding them as is recommended. And I learnt lots of other things besides. I was determined not to feel embarrassed like that again.

Maybe that girl did me a favour. Normally, no one ever remarks upon or points out poor table manners to us because it is bad manners to do so! Yet, our manners may be noted and may reflect poorly on us in certain circumstances.

Often, a breakfast, lunch, or dinner interview is part of process for higher executive jobs, especially where there is a lot of client contact. It gives the employer a chance to check out communication and interpersonal skills, as well as table manners, in a social environment removed from the office setting.

It's a key test for some employers who want to see their potential employees' social skills before they send them out into the world to represent the company.

If we don't know the basics in table manners, we may fail the interview without even realising why. Whether we like it or not, some people will perceive bad manners at the table as an indication that the person lacks education or is someone who cares more about the food than the company they're with.

That kind of judgement is unfair because we are taught from the time we're young that we don't wear pyjamas to mass for example, but most people are never taught simple guidelines on dining etiquette.

My nieces and nephews even rebelled because I have been so neurotic about making sure they never experienced the embarrassment I experienced. 'We're not coming out here to eat anymore because you're so annoying!' they said.

But for me, learning table manners is really about having respect for others around us.

And the real beauty about table manners is that everyone can have them because they don't cost a penny. Table manners are important because they are a courtesy to everyone at the table and a way to make others comfortable. I'm sure everyone else would rather not see me open my mouth when I am chewing my food, for example.

Also, if we are aware of the essential guidelines, we don't embarrass ourselves or others. Once we know our water and wine glasses are always placed to our right for example, it means we won't drink from someone else's glass.

Table manners are only common sense most of the time. However, common sense is not always as common as we think, so that is why there are a few 'rules'.

If we know a few basic guidelines, it means that we can feel more confident when we sit down at a table, whether we are sitting next to royalty or our granny.

If we know the 'rules', then dining out becomes easier and simpler, and what's wrong with feel happier and more relaxed in company?

The Guidelines

- When dining in an interview or business situation, select menu items that are easy to eat. Forget shellfish, fish that requires boning or any food that is distracting from the conversation.
- In the business situation, be conservative and choose red wine for meat and white wine for fish.
- Place the napkin on the lap upon seating.
- Refer to it as a napkin and not a 'serviette'.

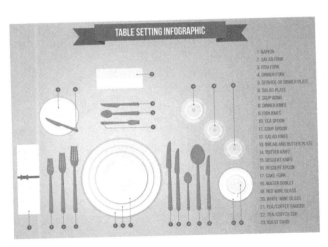

- We only start eating when everyone has been served and the host or hostess begins to eat. If we find we're halfway through our starter when the host says 'bon appétit' consider it a faux pas.

- Whether we're drinking from a white wine, red wine or champagne glass, we only ever hold a glass by the stem.
- Try not to make the same mistake I made by holding the knife and fork like a pen. The correct way to hold cutlery is with the handles tucked into the palms and the index finger extending down the back of the knife and the back side of the fork.
- The fork is held with the tines pointing downwards.
- Using the concave of a fork as a shovel to feed ourselves is frowned upon as is propelling any food to our mouth using a knife. Use the knife and fork simultaneously.

How to hold a knife and fork

- We are expected to raise the food to our mouths not lower our mouths to the food. It makes for better conversation when our faces are not in our plates!
- We always 'eat' soup and 'drink' tea.
- Never, ever slurp soup or tea.
- Soup is to be spooned away from us and the last of the soup is gathered by tilting the bowl away from us.
- We never, ever chew with our mouths open.

- We never mash food or cut up more than a couple of pieces at a time.
- We never, ever talk when there is food in our mouths.
- We place our cutlery on our plate (an inverted V-shape is recommended) to converse or to respond to a question.
- We never gesticulate with a knife and fork. As per the guidelines above, cutlery is placed on the plate before talking.
- When eating French bread or rolls, we break them with our fingers not a knife.
- We never butter the entire piece and bite off chunks. We place butter on our plate. Then we tear a piece of the bread with our hands, butter that piece, eat it and then repeat as necessary.
- When finished with soup, the spoon is left on the plate under the bowl.
- When sharing a sauce with others, we never dip our food into it. We spoon some of it on to our plate.
- Pass shared dishes from our left to our right. We serve ourselves and pass the dish on to our neighbours to the right. We are considerate and only take a small amount to ensure there is enough for everyone on the table.
- Pass jugs and gravy boats with the handle facing to the recipient.
- When we finish a course, we place the knife and fork parallel to each other, handles positioned at the bottom of our plate at around the four or five o'clock mark. The tines of the fork point upwards and the knife edge points in. This is a signal from bygone days to let servants know they could clear the plate. However, this message continues to work perfectly well today in all the best restaurants.

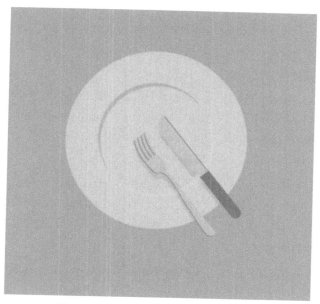

Placement of cutlery when finished a course

- At the end of the meal, we fold over our napkin and place it next to the left of the plate or place setting.
- The proper manner to drink tea at the table is to raise the tea cup, leaving the saucer on the table, and to place the cup back on the saucer between sips. No extended pinkies, please. We only carry both the cup and the saucer when we are standing.
- Big, noisy, circular stirring of tea is frowned upon. The 'proper' way to stir is to softly sway the spoon between the 12 o'clock position in the cup and the 6 o'clock position three or four times. When the tea spoon isn't being used, pop it back to the right of the cup on the saucer.

Note on American Versus European Dining Etiquette:

There is a difference in table manners and etiquette in America and Europe.

As Europeans, we keep the fork in our left hands and the knife in our right hand coaxes our food to our fork. The tines always remain facing downwards.

Americans cut a piece of their meat with a knife and fork, place the knife down, switch the fork to their right hands and then eat with the fork tines upwards. They begin the process all over again zig-zagging motion with their cutlery.

The American etiquette of putting the knife down after cutting harks back to the early 1700s when it was the custom in France. The French were the arbiters of taste for Americans of that era and the custom never changed.

It's said that American spies operating in Europe in the second World War were exposed because of this knife and fork switching habit!

ABOUT THE AUTHOR

Marion was born the eldest of five children of Denis and Sheila Goggin in Cork. She was educated in Upper Glanmire National School and Saint Vincent's Primary School before attending Miss O'Sullivan's (Miss O's).

Marion trained in beauty therapy in Jill Fisher's Beauty College in Dublin after leaving school.

As a young woman she fell in love and married Cork GAA star, Tom Creedon. Her happiness was short-lived when her husband died in

1983 after a freak accident. Marion was left a devastated young widow and a single mother to their baby, Tom.

She sought a new direction and new career path in life that would provide her with an income and let her continue to be a fulltime mum. While researching in Canada, she discovered a brand new and growing business in image consultancy. She went to London to study in colour analysis, image and style, and set up her own makeover business from her home in Cork becoming an international award-winning image consultant.

When her son Tom was eleven, Marion fell in love and married Cormac Hegarty, a property developer and became, Marion Creedon Hegarty.

He helped her develop and expand her business and she launched her own shops in Cork and Dublin. Soon after, she developed and manufactured her cosmetic and tan range, Top Image, which still sells in beauty salons and pharmacies around Ireland.

She opened a wholesale cash and carry premises at Fashion City in Dublin with 5,000 square feet of fashion accessories and her own cosmetics and tan range.

Still recovering from grief and depression, Marion also went back to education and studied a year-long programme in Social and Health with the Southern Health Board.

When she went for counselling to leading clinical psychologist and author, Doctor Tony Humphries, he recommended that she also study a two-year course in Interpersonal Communications in University College Cork.

Afterwards, she proceeded further and completed a level eight honours degree course in Relationship Mentoring in UCC.

Her business in image makeovers became more holistic and powerful as she included self-growth and personal development as part of her programme.

Marion was passionate about her work in life makeovers and coaching and continued successfully in the business for thirty-five years. She remains passionate about the wisdom and the insights that she has acquired in those years and about inspiring others to look and feel their best.

Now living in semi-retirement with Cormac in Reenaroga Island in West Cork, she has decided to write a book about her life, her healing and about how we can all make positive changes to our lives and become happier and better people.

To get in touch, you can email m.creedonhegarty@yahoo.ie or visit the Facebook page below.

facebook.com/marion.c.hegarty

Printed in Great Britain
by Amazon

80984236R20183